FOREWORD

The collection of "Everything Will Be Okay" travel phrasebooks published by T&P Books is designed for people traveling abroad for tourism and business. The phrasebooks contain what matters most - the essentials for basic communication. This is an indispensable set of phrases to "survive" while abroad.

This phrasebook will help you in most cases where you need to ask something, get directions, find out how much something costs, etc. It can also resolve difficult communication situations where gestures just won't help.

This book contains a lot of phrases that have been grouped according to the most relevant topics. A separate section of the book also provides a small dictionary with more than 1,500 important and useful words.

Take "Everything Will Be Okay" phrasebook with you on the road and you'll have an irreplaceable traveling companion who will help you find your way out of any situation and teach you to not fear speaking with foreigners.

TABLE OF CONTENTS

Pronunciation	5
List of abbreviations	7
English-Hindi	9
Concise Dictionary	75

T&P Books Publishing

PRONUNCIATION

Vowels

अ	अक्सर	[a]; [ɑ], [ə]	park; teacher
आ	आगमन	[a:]	calf, palm
इ	इनाम	[i]	shorter than in feet
ई	ईश्वर	[i], [i:]	feet, Peter
उ	उठना	[ʊ]	good, booklet
ऊ	ऊपर	[u:]	pool, room
ऋ	ऋग्वेद	[r, rʲ]	green
ए	एकता	[e:]	longer than in bell
ऐ	ऐनक	[aj]	time, white
ओ	ओला	[o:]	fall, bomb
औ	औरत	[au]	loud, powder
अं	अंजीर	[ŋ]	English, ring
अः	अ से अः	[h]	home, have
ऑ	ऑफिस	[ɒ]	cotton, pocket

Consonants

क	कमरा	[k]	clock, kiss
ख	खिड़की	[kh]	work hard
ग	गरज	[g]	game, gold
घ	घर	[gh]	g aspirated
ङ	डाकू	[n]	English, ring
च	चक्कर	[tʃ]	church, French
छ	छात्र	[tʃh]	hitchhiker
ज	जाना	[dʒ]	joke, general
झ	झलक	[dʒ]	joke, general
ञ	विज्ञान	[ɲ]	canyon, new
ट	मटर	[t]	tourist, trip
ठ	ठेका	[th]	don't have
ड	डंडा	[d]	day, doctor
ढ	ढलान	[d]	day, doctor
ण	क्षण	[n]	retroflex nasal
त	ताकत	[t]	tourist, trip

Letter	Hindi example	T&P phonetic alphabet	English example
थ	थकना	[th]	don't have
द	दरवाज़ा	[d]	day, doctor
ध	धोना	[d]	day, doctor
न	नाई	[n]	sang, thing
प	पिता	[p]	pencil, private
फ	फल	[f]	face, food
ब	बच्चा	[b]	baby, book
भ	भाई	[b]	baby, book
म	माता	[m]	magic, milk
य	याद	[j]	yes, New York
र	रीछ	[r]	rice, radio
ल	लाल	[l]	lace, people
व	वचन	[v]	very, river
श	शिक्षक	[ʃ]	machine, shark
ष	भाषा	[ʃ]	machine, shark
स	सोना	[s]	city, boss
ह	हज़ार	[h]	home, have

Additional consonants

क़	क़लम	[q]	king, club
ख़	ख़बर	[h]	huge, hat
ड़	लड़का	[r]	rice, radio
ढ़	पढ़ना	[r]	rice, radio
ग़	ग़लती	[ɣ]	between [g] and [h]
ज़	ज़िन्दगी	[z]	zebra, please
झ़	ट्रैझ़र	[ʒ]	forge, pleasure
फ़	फ़ौज	[f]	face, food

LIST OF ABBREVIATIONS

English abbreviations

ab.	-	about
adj	-	adjective
adv	-	adverb
anim.	-	animate
as adj	-	attributive noun used as adjective
e.g.	-	for example
etc.	-	et cetera
fam.	-	familiar
fem.	-	feminine
form.	-	formal
inanim.	-	inanimate
masc.	-	masculine
math	-	mathematics
mil.	-	military
n	-	noun
pl	-	plural
pron.	-	pronoun
sb	-	somebody
sing.	-	singular
sth	-	something
v aux	-	auxiliary verb
vi	-	intransitive verb
vi, vt	-	intransitive, transitive verb
vt	-	transitive verb

Hindi abbreviations

f	-	feminine noun
f pl	-	feminine plural
m	-	masculine noun
m pl	-	masculine plural

T&P BOOKS

HINDI
PHRASEBOOK

This section contains
important phrases that may
come in handy in various
real-life situations.
The phrasebook will help
you ask for directions, clarify
a price, buy tickets, and
order food at a restaurant

T&P Books Publishing

PHRASEBOOK CONTENTS

The bare minimum	12
Questions	15
Needs	16
Asking for directions	18
Signs	20
Transportation. General phrases	22
Buying tickets	24
Bus	26
Train	28
On the train. Dialogue (No ticket)	30
Taxi	31
Hotel	33
Restaurant	36
Shopping	38
In town	40
Money	42

Time   44
Greetings. Introductions   46
Farewells   48
Foreign language   50
Apologies   52
Agreement   53
Refusal. Expressing doubt   54
Expressing gratitude   56
Congratulations. Best wishes   57
Socializing   58
Sharing impressions. Emotions   61
Problems. Accidents   63
Health problems   66
At the pharmacy   69
The bare minimum   71

T&P Books Publishing

The bare minimum

Excuse me, ...	माफ़ कीजिएगा, ... māf kījiega, ...
Hello.	नमस्कार। namaskār.
Thank you.	शुक्रिया। shukriya.
Good bye.	अलविदा। alavida.
Yes.	हाँ। hān.
No.	नहीं। nahin.
I don't know.	मुझे नहीं मालूम। mujhe nahin mālūm.
Where? | Where to? | When?	कहाँ? | कहाँ जाना है? | कब? kahān? | kahān jāna hai? | kab?
I need ...	मुझे ... चाहिए। mujhe ... chāhie.
I want ...	मैं ... चाहता /चाहती/ हूँ। main ... chāhata /chāhatī/ hūn.
Do you have ...?	क्या आपके पास ... है? kya āpake pās ... hai?
Is there a ... here?	क्या यहाँ ... है? kya yahān ... hai?
May I ...?	क्या मैं ... सकता /सकती/ हूँ? kya main ... sakata /sakatī/ hūn?
..., please (polite request)	..., कृपया। ..., krpaya.
I'm looking for ...	मैं ... ढूंढ रहा /रही/ हूँ। main ... dhūnrh raha /rahī/ hūn.
restroom	शौचालय shauchālay
ATM	एटीएम etīem
pharmacy (drugstore)	दवा की दुकान dava kī dukān
hospital	अस्पताल aspatāl
police station	पुलिस थाना pulis thāna
subway	मेट्रो metro

taxi	टैक्सी taiksī
train station	ट्रेन स्टेशन tren steshan

My name is ...	मेरा नाम ... है। mera nām ... hai
What's your name?	आपका क्या नाम है? āpaka kya nām hai?
Could you please help me?	क्या आप मेरी मदद कर सकते /सकती/ हैं? kya āp merī madad kar sakate /sakatī/ hain?
I've got a problem.	मुझे एक परेशानी है। mujhe ek pareshānī hai.
I don't feel well.	मेरी तबियत ठीक नहीं है। merī tabiyat thīk nahin hai.
Call an ambulance!	एम्बुलेन्स बुलाओ! embulens bulao!
May I make a call?	क्या मैं एक फ़ोन कर सकता /सकती/ हूँ? kya main ek fon kar sakata /sakatī/ hūn?

I'm sorry.	मुझे माफ़ करना। mujhe māf kar do.
You're welcome.	आपका स्वागत है। āpaka svāgat hai.

I, me	मैं main
you (inform.)	तू tu
he	वह vah
she	वह vah
they (masc.)	वे ve
they (fem.)	वे ve
we	हम ham
you (pl)	तुम tum
you (sg, form.)	आप āp

ENTRANCE	प्रवेश pravesh
EXIT	निकास nikās

OUT OF ORDER	ख़राब है kharāb hai
CLOSED	बंद band
OPEN	खुला khula
FOR WOMEN	महिलाओं के लिए mahilaon ke lie
FOR MEN	पुरूषों के लिए purūshon ke lie

Questions

Where?	कहाँ? kahān?
Where to?	कहाँ जाना है? kahān jāna hai?
Where from?	कहाँ से? kahān se?
Why?	क्यों? kyon?
For what reason?	किस वजह से? kis vajah se?
When?	कब? kab?
How long?	कितना समय लगेगा? kitana samay lagega?
At what time?	कितने बजे? kitane baje?
How much?	कितना? kitana?
Do you have ...?	क्या आपके पास ... है? kya āpake pās ... hai?
Where is ...?	... कहाँ है? ... kahān hai?
What time is it?	क्या बजा है? kya baja hai?
May I make a call?	क्या मैं एक फ़ोन कर सकता /सकती/ हूँ? kya main ek fon kar sakata /sakatī/ hūn?
Who's there?	कौन है? kaun hai?
Can I smoke here?	क्या मैं यहाँ सिगरेट पी सकता /सकती/ हूँ? kya main yahān sigaret pī sakata /sakatī/ hūn?
May I ...?	क्या मैं ... सकता /सकती/ हूँ? kya main ... sakata /sakatī/ hūn?

Needs

I'd like ...	मुझे ... चाहिए। mujhe ... chāhie.
I don't want ...	मुझे ... नहीं चाहिए। mujhe ... nahin chāhie.
I'm thirsty.	मुझे प्यास लगी है। mujhe pyās lagī hai.
I want to sleep.	मैं सोना चाहता /चाहती/ हूँ। main sona chāhata /chāhatī/ hūn.
I want ...	मैं ... चाहता /चाहती/ हूँ। main ... chāhata /chāhatī/ hūn.
to wash up	हाथ-मुँह धोना hāth-munh dhona
to brush my teeth	दाँत ब्रश करना dānt brash karana
to rest a while	कुछ समय आराम करना kuchh samay ārām karana
to change my clothes	कपड़े बदलना kapare badalana
to go back to the hotel	होटल वापस जाना hotal vāpas jāna
to buy ...	... खरीदना ... kharīdana
to go to ...	... जाना ... jāna
to visit ...	... जाना ... jāna
to meet with ...	... से मिलने जाना ... se milane jāna
to make a call	फ़ोन करना fon karana
I'm tired.	मैं थक गया /गई/ हूँ। main thak gaya /gaī/ hūn.
We are tired.	हम थक गए हैं। ham thak gae hain.
I'm cold.	मुझे सर्दी लग रही है। mujhe sardī lag rahī hai.
I'm hot.	मुझे गर्मी लग रही है। mujhe garmī lag rahī hai.
I'm OK.	मैं ठीक हूँ। main thīk hūn.

I need to make a call.

मुझे फ़ोन करना है।
mujhe fon karana hai.

I need to go to the restroom.

मुझे शौचालय जाना है।
mujhe shauchālay jāna hai.

I have to go.

मुझे जाना है।
mujhe jāna hoga.

I have to go now.

मुझे अब जाना होगा।
mujhe ab jāna hoga.

Asking for directions

Excuse me, …	माफ़ कीजिएगा, … māf kījiega, …
Where is …?	… कहाँ है? … kahān hai?
Which way is …?	… कहाँ पड़ेगा? … kahān parega?
Could you help me, please?	क्या आप मेरी मदद करेंगे /करेंगी/, प्लीज़? kya āp merī madad karenge /karengī/, plīz?
I'm looking for …	मैं … ढूँढ रहा /रही/ हूँ। main … dhūnrh raha /rahī/ hūn.
I'm looking for the exit.	मैं बाहर निकलने का रास्ता ढूँढ रहा /रही/ हूँ। main bāhar nikalane ka rāsta dhūnrh raha /rahī/ hūn.
I'm going to …	मैं … जा रहा /रही/ हूँ। main … ja raha /rahī/ hūn.
Am I going the right way to …?	क्या मैं …जाने के लिए सही रास्ते पर हूँ? kya main … jāne ke lie sahī rāste par hūn?
Is it far?	क्या वह दूर है? kya vah dūr hai?
Can I get there on foot?	क्या मैं वहाँ पैदल जा सकता /सकती/ हूँ? kya main vahān paidal ja sakata /sakatī/ hūn?
Can you show me on the map?	क्या आप मुझे नक़्शे पर दिखा सकते /सकती/ हैं? kya āp mujhe nakshe par dikha sakate /sakatī/ hain?
Show me where we are right now.	मुझे दिखाईये कि हम इस वक्त कहाँ है। mujhe dikhaīye ki ham is vakt kahān hain.
Here	यहाँ yahān
There	वहाँ vahān
This way	इस तरफ़ is taraf

Turn right.   **दायें मुड़ें।**
dāyen muren.

Turn left.   **बायें मुड़ें।**
bāyen muren.

first (second, third) turn   **पहला (दूसरा, तीसरा) मोड़**
pahala (dūsara, tīsara) mor

to the right   **दाईं ओर**
daīn or

to the left   **बाईं ओर**
baīn or

Go straight ahead.   **सीधे जाएं।**
sīdhe jaen.

Signs

WELCOME!	स्वागत! svāgat!
ENTRANCE	प्रवेश pravesh
EXIT	निकास nikās
PUSH	पुश, धकेलिए push, dhakelie
PULL	पुल, खींचिए pul, khīnchie
OPEN	खुला khula
CLOSED	बंद band
FOR WOMEN	महिलाओं के लिए mahilaon ke lie
FOR MEN	पुरूषों के लिए purūshon ke lie
GENTLEMEN, GENTS (m)	पुरूष purūsh
WOMEN (f)	महिलाएं mahilaen
DISCOUNTS	छूट chhūt
SALE	सेल sel
FREE	मुफ्त muft
NEW!	नया! naya!
ATTENTION!	ध्यान दें! dhyān den!
NO VACANCIES	कोई कमरा खाली नहीं है koī naukarī nahin hai
RESERVED	रिज़र्वड rizarvad
ADMINISTRATION	प्रबंधन prabandhan
STAFF ONLY	केवल स्टाफ़ keval stāf

BEWARE OF THE DOG!	कुत्ते से बचकर रहें! kutte se bachakar rahen!
NO SMOKING!	नो स्मोकिंग! no smoking!
DO NOT TOUCH!	हाथ न लगाएं! hāth na lagaen!
DANGEROUS	खतरनाक khataranāk
DANGER	खतरा khatara
HIGH VOLTAGE	हाई वोल्टेज haī voltej
NO SWIMMING!	स्वीमिंग की अनुमति नहीं है! svīming kī anumati nahin hai!
OUT OF ORDER	ख़राब है kharāb hai
FLAMMABLE	ज्वलनशील jvalanashīl
FORBIDDEN	मनाही manāhī
NO TRESPASSING!	प्रवेश निषेध! yahān āne kī sakht manāhī hai!
WET PAINT	गीला पेंट gīla pent
CLOSED FOR RENOVATIONS	मरम्मत के लिए बंद marammat ke lie band
WORKS AHEAD	आगे कार्य प्रगित पर है āge kāry pragit par hai
DETOUR	डीटूर dītur

Transportation. General phrases

plane	हवाई जहाज़ havaī jahāz
train	रेलगाड़ी, ट्रेन relagāṛī, tren
bus	बस bas
ferry	फेरी ferī
taxi	टैक्सी taiksī
car	कार kār

schedule	शिड्यूल shidyūl
Where can I see the schedule?	मैं शिड्यूल कहां देख सकता /सकती/ हूं? main shidyūl kahān dekh sakata /sakatī/ hūn?

workdays (weekdays)	कार्यदिवस kāryadivas
weekends	समाहांत saptāhānt
holidays	छुट्टियां chhuttiyān

DEPARTURE	प्रस्थान prasthān
ARRIVAL	आगमन āgaman
DELAYED	देरी derī
CANCELLED	रद्द radd

next (train, etc.)	अगला agala
first	पहला pahala
last	अंतिम antim

When is the next ...?

अगला ... कब है?
agala ... kab hai?

When is the first ...?

पहला ... कब है?
pahala ... kab hai?

When is the last ...?

अंतिम ... कब है?
antim ... kab hai?

---

transfer (change of trains, etc.)

ट्रेन बदलना
tren badalana

to make a transfer

ट्रेन कैसे बदलें
tren kaise badalen

Do I need to make a transfer?

क्या मुझे ट्रेन बदलनी पड़गी?
kya mujhe tren badalani paragi?

Buying tickets

Where can I buy tickets?	मैं टिकटें कुहाँ खरीद सकता /सकती/ हूँ? main tikaten kahān kharīd sakata /sakatī/ hūn?
ticket	टिकट tikat
to buy a ticket	टिकट खरीदना tikat kharīdana
ticket price	टिकट का दाम tikat ka dām
Where to?	कहाँ जाना है? kahān jāna hai?
To what station?	कौन-से स्टेशन के लिए? kaun-se steshan ke lie?
I need ...	मुझे ... चाहिए. mujhe ... chāhie.
one ticket	एक टिकट ek tikat
two tickets	दो टिकट do tikat
three tickets	तीन टिकट tīn tikat
one-way	एक तरफ़ ek taraf
round-trip	राउंड ट्रिप raund trip
first class	फर्स्ट क्लास farst klās
second class	सेकेंड क्लास sekend klās
today	आज āj
tomorrow	कल kal
the day after tomorrow	कल के बाद वाला दिन kal ke bād vāla din
in the morning	सुबह में subah men
in the afternoon	दोपहर में dopahar men
in the evening	शाम में shām men

aisle seat

आयल सीट
āyal sīt

window seat

खिड़की वाली सीट
khirakī vālī sīt

How much?

कितना?
kitana?

Can I pay by credit card?

क्या मैं क्रेडिट कार्ड से पे कर
सकता /सकती/ हूँ?
kya main kredit kārd se pe kar
sakata /sakatī/ hūn?

Bus

bus	बस bas
intercity bus	अंतरराज्यीय बस antararājyīy bas
bus stop	बस-स्टॉप bas-stop
Where's the nearest bus stop?	सबसे करीबी बस-स्टॉप कहाँ है? sabase karībī bas-stop kahān hai?
number (bus ~, etc.)	नंबर nambar
Which bus do I take to get to ...?	... जाने के लिए कौन-सी बस लेनी होगी? ... jāne ke lie kaun-sī bas lenī hogī?
Does this bus go to ...?	क्या यह बस ... जाती है? kya yah bas ... jātī hai?
How frequent are the buses?	बसें कितनी जल्दी-जल्दी आती हैं? basen kitanī jaldī-jaldī ātī hain?
every 15 minutes	हर पंद्रह मिनट har pandrah minat
every half hour	हर आधा घंटा har ādha ghanta
every hour	हर घंटा har ghanta
several times a day	दिन में कई बार din men kaī bār
... times a day	दिन में ... बार din men ... bār
schedule	शिड्यूल shidyūl
Where can I see the schedule?	मैं शिड्यूल कहाँ देख सकता /सकती/ हूँ? main shidyūl kahān dekh sakata /sakatī/ hūn?
When is the next bus?	अगली बस कब है? agalī bas kab hai?
When is the first bus?	पहली बस कब है? pahalī bas kab hai?
When is the last bus?	आखिरी बस कब है? ākhirī bas kab hai?

stop

स्टॉप
stop

next stop

अगला स्टॉप
agala stop

last stop (terminus)

आखिरी स्टॉप
ākhirī stop

Stop here, please.

रोक दें, प्लीज़।
yahān roken, plīz.

Excuse me, this is my stop.

माफ़ कीजिएगा, यह मेरा स्टॉप है।
māf kījiega, yah mera stop hai.

Train

train	रेलगाड़ी, ट्रेन relagāṛī, tren
suburban train	लोकल ट्रेन lokal tren
long-distance train	लंबी दूरी की ट्रेन lambī dūrī kī tren

train station	ट्रेन स्टेशन tren steshan
Excuse me, where is the exit to the platform?	माफ़ कीजिएगा, प्लेटफॉर्म से निकलने का रास्ता कहाँ है? māf kījiega, pletaform se nikalane ka rāsta kahān hai?

Does this train go to ...?	क्या यह ट्रेन ... जाती है? kya yah tren ... jātī hai?
next train	अगली ट्रेन agalī tren
When is the next train?	अगली ट्रेन कब है? agalī tren kab hai?

Where can I see the schedule?	मैं शिड्यूल कहाँ देख सकता /सकती/ हूँ? main shidyūl kahān dekh sakata /sakatī/ hūn?
From which platform?	कौन-से प्लेटफॉर्म से? kaun-se pletaform se?
When does the train arrive in ...?	... में ट्रेन कब पहुंचती है? ... men tren kab pahunchatī hai?

Please help me.	कृपया मेरी मदद करें। kṛpaya merī madad karen.
I'm looking for my seat.	मैं अपनी सीट ढूंढ रहा /रही/ हूँ। main apanī sīṭ dhūnrh raha /rahī/ hūn.
We're looking for our seats.	हम अपनी सीट ढूंढ रहे हैं। ham apanī sīṭ dhūnrh rahe hain.

My seat is taken.	मेरी सीट पर कोई और बैठा है। merī sīṭ par koī aur baitha hai.
Our seats are taken.	हमारी सीटों पर कोई और बैठा है। hamārī sīṭon par koī aur baitha hai.
I'm sorry but this is my seat.	माफ़ कीजिएगा, लेकिन यह मेरी सीट है। māf kījiega, lekin yah merī sīṭ hai.

Is this seat taken?

क्या इस सीट पर कोई बैठा है?
kya is sīt par koī baitha hai?

May I sit here?

क्या मैं यहाँ बैठ सकता
/सकती/ हूँ?
kya main yahān baith sakata
/sakatī/ hūn?

On the train. Dialogue (No ticket)

Ticket, please.
टिकट, कृपया।
tikat, krpāya.

I don't have a ticket.
मेरे पास टिकट नहीं है।
mere pās tikat nahin hai.

I lost my ticket.
मेरा टिकट खो गया।
mera tikat kho gaya.

I forgot my ticket at home.
मैं अपना टिकट घर पर भूल गया /गई/।
main apana tikat ghar par bhūl gaya /gaī/.

You can buy a ticket from me.
आप मुझे एक टिकट दे दें।
āp mujhe ek tikat de den.

You will also have to pay a fine.
आपको फाइन भी भरना होगा।
āpako fain bhī bharana hoga.

Okay.
ठीक है।
thīk hai.

Where are you going?
आप कहाँ जा रहे /रही/ हैं?
āp kahān ja rahe /rahī/ hain?

I'm going to ...
मैं ... जा रहा /रही/ हूँ।
main ... ja raha /rahī/ hūn.

How much? I don't understand.
कितना? मैं समझी /समझी/ नहीं।
kitana? main samajhī /samajhī/ nahin.

Write it down, please.
इसे लिख दीजिए, प्लीज़।
ise likh dījie, plīz.

Okay. Can I pay with a credit card?
ठीक है। क्या मैं क्रेडिट कार्ड से पे कर सकता /सकती/ हूँ?
thīk hai. kya main kredit kārd se pe kar sakata /sakatī/ hūn?

Yes, you can.
हाँ, आप कर सकते हैं।
hān, āp kar sakate hain.

Here's your receipt.
यह रही आपकी रसीद।
yah rahī āpakī rasīd.

Sorry about the fine.
फाइन के बारे में माफ़ कीजिएगा।
fain ke bāre men māf kījiega.

That's okay. It was my fault.
कोई बात नहीं। वह मेरी गलती थी।
koī bāt nahin. vah merī galatī thī.

Enjoy your trip.
अपनी यात्रा का आनंद लें।
apanī yātra ka ānand len.

Taxi

taxi	टैक्सी taiksī
taxi driver	टैक्सी चलाने वाला taiksī chalāne vāla
to catch a taxi	टैक्सी पकड़ना taiksī pakarana
taxi stand	टैक्सी स्टैंड taiksī staind
Where can I get a taxi?	मुझे टैक्सी कहां मिलेगी? mujhe taiksī kahān milegī?
to call a taxi	टैक्सी बुलाना taiksī bulāna
I need a taxi.	मुझे टैक्सी चाहिए। mujhe taiksī chāhie.
Right now.	अभी। abhī.
What is your address (location)?	आपका पता क्या है? āpaka pata kya hai?
My address is ...	मेरा पता है ... mera pata hai ...
Your destination?	आपको कहाँ जाना है? āpako kahān jāna hai?
Excuse me, ...	माफ़ कीजिएगा, ... māf kījiega, ...
Are you available?	क्या टैक्सी खाली है? kya taiksī khālī hai?
How much is it to get to ...?	... जाने के लिए कितना लगेगा? ... jāne ke lie kitana lagega?
Do you know where it is?	क्या आपको पता है वह कहाँ है? kya āpako pata hai vah kahān hai?
Airport, please.	एयरपोर्ट, प्लीज़ा eyaraport, plīz.
Stop here, please.	यहाँ रोकें, प्लीज़ा rok den, plīz.
It's not here.	यहाँ नहीं है। yahān nahin hai.
This is the wrong address.	यह गलत पता है। yah galat pata hai.
Turn left.	बायें मुड़ें। bāyen muren.

Turn right.

दायें मुड़ें

dāyen muren.

How much do I owe you?

मुझे आपको कितने पैसे देने हैं?

mujhe āpako kitane paise dene hain?

I'd like a receipt, please.

मैं एक रसीद चाहिए, प्लीज़ा

main ek rasīd chāhie, plīz.

Keep the change.

छुट्टे रख लें

chhutte rakh len.

Would you please wait for me?

क्या आप मेरा इंतज़ार /करेंगे/ करेंगी?

kya āp mera intazār /karenge/ karengī?

five minutes

पाँच मिनट

pānch minat

ten minutes

दस मिनट

das minat

fifteen minutes

पंद्रह मिनट

pandrah minat

twenty minutes

बीस मिनट

bīs minat

half an hour

आधा घंटा

ādhe ghante

Hotel

Hello.	नमस्कार। namaskār.
My name is ...	मेरा नाम ... है mera nām ... hai
I have a reservation.	मैंने बुकिंग की थी। mainne buking kī thī.
I need ...	मुझे ... चाहिए। mujhe ... chāhie.
a single room	एक सिंगल कमरा ek singal kamara
a double room	एक डबल कमरा ek dabal kamara
How much is that?	यह कितने का है? yah kitane ka hai?
That's a bit expensive.	यह थोड़ा महंगा है। yah thora mahanga hai.
Do you have anything else?	क्या आपके पास कुछ और है? kya āpake pās kuchh aur hai?
I'll take it.	मैं यह ले लूँगा /लूँगी/। main yah le lūnga /lūngī/.
I'll pay in cash.	मैं नकद दूंगा /दूँगी/। main nakad dūnga /dūngī/.
I've got a problem.	मुझे एक परेशानी है। mujhe ek pareshānī hai.
My ... is broken.	मेरा ... टूटा हुआ है। mera ... tūta hua hai.
My ... is out of order.	मेरा ... ख़राब है। mera ... kharāb hai.
TV	टीवी tīvī
air conditioner	एयरकंडिशनर eyarakandishanar
tap	नल nal
shower	शॉवर shovar
sink	बेसिन besin
safe	तिजोरी tijorī

door lock	दरवाज़े का ताला daravāze ka tāla
electrical outlet	सॉकेट soket
hairdryer	हेयर ड्रायर heyar drāyar

I don't have …	… नहीं है … nahin hai
water	पानी pānī
light	लाइट lait
electricity	बिजली bijalī

Can you give me …?	… दे सकते /सकती/ हैं? de sakate /sakatī/ hain?
a towel	तौलिया tauliya
a blanket	कम्बल kambal
slippers	चप्पल chappal
a robe	रोब rob
shampoo	शैम्पू shaimpū
soap	साबुन sābun

I'd like to change rooms.	मुझे अपना कमरा बदलना है। mujhe apana kamara badalana hai.
I can't find my key.	मुझे चाबी नहीं मिल रही है। mujhe chābī nahin mil rahī hai.
Could you open my room, please?	क्या आप मेरा कमरा खोल सकते /सकती/ हैं? kya āp mera kamara khol sakate /sakatī/ hain?

Who's there?	कौन है? kaun hai?
Come in!	अंदर आ जाओ! andar ā jao!
Just a minute!	एक मिनट! ek minat!

Not right now, please.	अभी नहीं, प्लीज़। abhī nahin, plīz.
Come to my room, please.	कृपया मेरे कमरे में आईये। krpaya mere kamare men āīye.

I'd like to order food service.

मैं फ़ूड सर्विस ऑर्डर करना चाहता /चाहती/ हूँ।
main fūd sarvis ordar karana chāhata /chāhatī/ hūn.

My room number is ...

मेरा कमरा नंबर है ...
mera kamara nambar hai ...

I'm leaving ...

मैं ... जा रहा /रही/ हूँ।
main ... ja raha /rahī/ hūn.

We're leaving ...

हम ... जा रहे हैं।
ham ... ja rahe hain.

right now

अभी
abhī

this afternoon

आज दोपहर
āj dopahar

tonight

आज रात
āj rāt

tomorrow

कल
kal

tomorrow morning

कल सुबह
kal subah

tomorrow evening

कल शाम
kal shām

the day after tomorrow

कल के बाद वाला दिन
kal ke bād vāla din

I'd like to pay.

मैं भुगतान करना चाहता /चाहती/ हूँ।
main bhugatān karana chāhata /chāhatī/ hūn.

Everything was wonderful.

सब कुछ बहुत अच्छा था।
sab kuchh bahut achchha tha.

Where can I get a taxi?

मुझे टैक्सी कहां मिलेगी?
mujhe taiksī kahān milegī?

Would you call a taxi for me, please?

क्या आप मेरे लिए एक टैक्सी बुला देंगे /देंगी/?
kya āp mere lie ek taiksī bula denge /dengī/?

Restaurant

Can I look at the menu, please?
क्या आप अपना मेनू दिखा सकते हैं, प्लीज़?
kya āp apana menū dikha sakate hain, plīz?

Table for one.
एक के लिए टेबला
ek ke lie tebal.

There are two (three, four) of us.
हम दो (तीन, चार) लोग हैं
ham do (tīn, chār) log hain.

Smoking
स्मोकिंग
smoking

No smoking
नो स्मोकिंग
no smoking

Excuse me! (addressing a waiter)
एक्सक्यूज़ मी!
eksakyūz mī!

menu
मेनू
menū

wine list
वाइन सूची
vain sūchī

The menu, please.
मेनू ले आईये प्लीज़।
menū le āīye plīz.

Are you ready to order?
क्या आप ऑर्डर करने के लिए तैयार हैं?
kya āp ordar karane ke lie taiyār hain?

What will you have?
आप क्या लेना चाहेंगी /चाहेंगी/?
āp kya lena chāhengī /chāhengī/?

I'll have ...
मेरे लिए ... ले आईए
mere lie ... le āīe.

I'm a vegetarian.
मैं शाकाहारी हूँ
main shākāhārī hūn.

meat
माँस
māns

fish
मछली
machhalī

vegetables
सब्जियाँ
sabziyān

Do you have vegetarian dishes?
क्या आपके पास शाकाहारी पकवान हैं?
kya āpake pās shākāhārī pakavān hain?

I don't eat pork.
मैं सूअर का गोश्त नहीं खाता /खाती/ हूँ
main sūar ka gosht nahin khāta /khātī/ hūn.

He /she/ doesn't eat meat.

वह माँस नहीं खाता /खाती/ है।
vah māns nahin khāta /khātī/ hai.

I am allergic to ...

मुझे ... से अलर्जी है।
mujhe ... se alarjī hai.

Would you please bring me ...

क्या आप मेरे लिए ... ले आएंगे प्लीज़
kya āp mere lie ... le āenge plīz

salt | pepper | sugar

नमक | काली मिर्च | चीनी
namak | kālī mirch | chīnī

coffee | tea | dessert

कॉफ़ी | चाय | मीठा
kofī | chāy | mītha

water | sparkling | plain

पानी | बुदबुदाने वाला पानी | सादा
pānī | budabudāne vāla pānī | sāda

a spoon | fork | knife

एक चम्मच | काँटा | चाकू
ek chammach | kānta | chākū

a plate | napkin

एक प्लेट | नैपकिन
ek plet | naipakin

Enjoy your meal!

अपने भोजन का आनंद लें!
apane bhojan ka ānand len!

One more, please.

एक और चाहिए।
ek aur chāhie.

It was very delicious.

वह अत्यंत स्वादिष्ट था।
vah atyant svādisht tha.

check | change | tip

चेक | छुट्टा | टिप
chek | chhutta | tip

Check, please.
(Could I have the check, please?)

चेक प्लीज़।
chek plīz.

Can I pay by credit card?

क्या मैं क्रेडिट कार्ड से पे कर
सकता /सकती/ हूँ?
kya main kredit kārd se pe kar sakata
/sakatī/ hūn?

I'm sorry, there's a mistake here.

माफ़ कीजिएगा, यहाँ कुछ गलती है।
māf kījiega, yahān kuchh galatī hai.

Shopping

Can I help you? क्या मैं आपकी मदद कर सकता /सकती/ हूँ?
kya main āpakī madad kar sakata /sakatī/ hūn?

Do you have ...? क्या आपके पास ... है?
kya āpake pās ... hai?

I'm looking for ... मैं ... ढूंढ रहा /रही/ हूँ
main ... dhūnrh raha /rahī/ hūn.

I need ... मुझे ... चाहिए
mujhe ... chāhie.

I'm just looking. मैं बस देख रहा /रही/ हूँ
main bas dekh raha /rahī/ hūn.

We're just looking. हम बस देख रहे हैं
ham bas dekh rahe hain.

I'll come back later. मैं बाद में वापिस आता /आती/ हूँ
main bād men vāpis āta /ātī/ hūn.

We'll come back later. हम बाद में वापिस आते हैं
ham bād men vāpis āte hain.

discounts | sale छूट | सेल
chhūt | sel

Would you please show me ... क्या आप मुझे ... दिखाएंगे /दिखाएंगी/
kya āp mujhe ... dikhaenge /dikhaengī/.

Would you please give me ... क्या आप मुझे ... देंगे /देंगी/
kya āp mujhe ... denge /dengī/.

Can I try it on? क्या मैं इसे पहनकर देख सकता /सकती/ हूँ?
kya main ise pahanakar dekh sakata /sakatī/ hūn?

Excuse me, where's the fitting room? माफ़ कीजिएगा, ट्राय रूम कहाँ है?
māf kījiega, trāy rūm kahān hai?

Which color would you like? आपको कौन-सा रंग चाहिए?
āpako kaun-sa rang chāhie?

size | length साइज़ | लंबाई
saiz | lambaī

How does it fit? यह कैसा फिट होता है?
yah kaisa fit hota hai?

How much is it? यह कितने का है?
yah kitane ka hai?

That's too expensive. यह बहुत महंगा है
yah bahut mahanga hai.

I'll take it.

मैं इसे ले लूँगा /लूँगी/।
main ise le lūnga /lūngī/.

Excuse me, where do I pay?

माफ़ कीजिएगा, पे कहाँ करना है?
māf kījiega, pe kahān karana hai?

Will you pay in cash or credit card?

क्या आप नकद में पे करेंगे या क्रेडिट कार्ड से?
kya āp nakad men pe karenge ya kredit kārd se?

In cash | with credit card

नकद में | क्रेडिट कार्ड से
nakad men | kredit kārd se

Do you want the receipt?

क्या आपको रसीद चाहिए?
kya āpako rasīd chāhie?

Yes, please.

हाँ, प्लीज़।
hān, plīz.

No, it's OK.

नहीं, ज़रूरत नहीं।
nahin, zarūrat nahin.

Thank you. Have a nice day!

शुक्रिया। आपका दिन शुभ हो!
shukriya. āpaka din shubh ho!

In town

Excuse me, please.	माफ़ कीजिएगा, ... māf kījiega, ...
I'm looking for ...	मैं ... ढूंढ रहा /रही/ हूँ। main ... dhūnrh raha /rahī/ hūn.
the subway	मेट्रो metro
my hotel	अपना होटल apana hotal
the movie theater	सिनेमा हॉल sinema hol
a taxi stand	टैक्सी स्टैंड taiksī staind
an ATM	एटीएम etīem
a foreign exchange office	मुद्रा विनिमय केंद्र fŏran eksachenj ofis
an internet café	साइबर कैफ़े saibar kaife
... street	... सड़क ... sarak
this place	यह जगह yah jagah
Do you know where ... is?	क्या आपको पता है कि ... कहाँ है? kya āpako pata hai ki ... kahān hai?
Which street is this?	यह कौन-सी सड़क है? yah kaun-sī sarak hai?
Show me where we are right now.	मुझे दिखाईये कि हम इस वक्त कहाँ है। mujhe dikhaīye ki ham is vakt kahān hain.
Can I get there on foot?	क्या मैं वहाँ पैदल जा सकता /सकती/ हूँ? kya main vahān paidal ja sakata /sakatī/ hūn?
Do you have a map of the city?	क्या आपके पास शहर का नक्शा है? kya āpake pās shahar ka naksha hai?
How much is a ticket to get in?	अंदर जाने का टिकट कितने का है? andar jāne ka tikat kitane ka hai?
Can I take pictures here?	क्या मैं यहाँ फोटो खींच सकता /सकती/ हूँ? kya main yahān foto khīnch sakata /sakatī/ hūn?

Are you open?

क्या यह जगह खुली है?
kya yah jagah khulī hai?

When do you open?

आप इसे कब खोलते हैं?
āp ise kab kholate hain?

When do you close?

आप इसे कब बंद करते हैं?
āp ise kab band karate hain?

Money

money	पैसा paisa
cash	नकद nakad
paper money	पेपर मनी pepar manī
loose change	सिक्के sikke
check | change | tip	चेक | छुट्टा | टिप chek | chhutta | tip
credit card	क्रेडिट कार्ड kredit kārd
wallet	बटुआ batua
to buy	खरीदना kharīdana
to pay	भुगतान करना bhugatān karana
fine	फाइन fain
free	मुफ्त muft
Where can I buy ...?	मैं ... कहा खरीद सकता /सकती/ हूँ? main ... kaha kharīd sakata /sakatī/ hūn?
Is the bank open now?	क्या बैंक इस वक्त खुला होगा? kya baink is vakt khula hoga?
When does it open?	वह कब खुलता है? vah kab khulata hai?
When does it close?	वह कब बंद होता है? vah kab band hota hai?
How much?	कितना? kitana?
How much is this?	यह कितने का है? yah kitane ka hai?
That's too expensive.	यह बहुत महंगा है yah bahut mahanga hai.
Excuse me, where do I pay?	माफ़ कीजिएगा, पे कहाँ करना है? māf kījiega, pe kahān karana hai?

Check, please.

चेक, प्लीज़ा
chek, plīz.

Can I pay by credit card?

क्या मैं क्रेडिट कार्ड से पे कर सकता /सकती/ हूँ?
kya main kredit kārd se pe kar sakata /sakatī/ hūn?

Is there an ATM here?

क्या यहाँ पास में एटीएम है?
kya yahān pās men etīem hai?

I'm looking for an ATM.

मैं एटीएम ढूंढ रहा /रही/ हूँ
main etīem dhūnrh raha /rahī/ hūn.

I'm looking for a foreign exchange office.

मैं मुद्रा विनिमय केंद्र ढूंढ रहा /रही/ हूँ
main mudra vinimay kendr dhūnrh raha /rahī/ hūn.

I'd like to change ...

मैं ... बदलना चाहूँगा /चाहूँगी/।
main ... badalana chāhūngā /chāhūngī/.

What is the exchange rate?

एक्सचेंज रेट क्या है?
eksachenj ret kya hai?

Do you need my passport?

क्या मुझे पासपोर्ट की ज़रूरत है?
kya mujhe pāsaport kī zarūrat hai?

Time

What time is it?	क्या बजा है? kya baja hai?
When?	कब? kab?
At what time?	कितने बजे? kitane baje?
now | later | after …	अभी | बाद में | … के बाद abhī | bād men | … ke bād
one o'clock	एक बजे ek baje
one fifteen	सवा एक बजे sava ek baje
one thirty	डेढ़ बजे derh baje
one forty-five	पौने दो बजे paune do baje
one | two | three	एक | दो | तीन ek | do | tīn
four | five | six	चार | पांच | छह chār | pānch | chhah
seven | eight | nine	सात | आठ | नौ sāt | āth | nau
ten | eleven | twelve	दस | ग्यारह | बारह das | gyārah | bārah
in …	… में … men
five minutes	पाँच मिनट pānch minat
ten minutes	दस मिनट das minat
fifteen minutes	पंद्रह मिनट pandrah minat
twenty minutes	बीस मिनट bīs minat
half an hour	आधे घंटे ādha ghanta
an hour	एक घंटे ek ghante
in the morning	सुबह में subah men
early in the morning	सुबह-सेवरे subah-sevare

this morning	इस सुबह is subah
tomorrow morning	कल सुबह kal subah
in the middle of the day	दोपहर में dopahar men
in the afternoon	दोपहर में dopahar men
in the evening	शाम में shām men
tonight	आज रात āj rāt
at night	रात को rāt ko
yesterday	कल kal
today	आज āj
tomorrow	कल kal
the day after tomorrow	कल के बाद वाला दिन kal ke bād vāla din
What day is it today?	आज कौन-सा दिन है? āj kaun-sa din hai?
It's ...	आज ... है। āj ... hai.
Monday	सोमवार somavār
Tuesday	मंगलवार mangalavār
Wednesday	बुधवार budhavār
Thursday	गुरुवार guruvār
Friday	शुक्रवार shukravār
Saturday	शनिवार shanivār
Sunday	रविवार ravivār

Greetings. Introductions

Hello.

नमस्कार
namaskār.

Pleased to meet you.

आपसे मिलकर ख़ुशी हुई
āpase milakar khushī huī.

Me too.

मुझे भी
mujhe bhī.

I'd like you to meet ...

मैं आपको ... से मिलाना चाहूँगा
/चाहूँगी/।
main āpako ... se milāna chāhūnga
/chāhūngī/.

Nice to meet you.

आपसे मिलकर अच्छा लगा
āpase milakar achchha laga.

How are you?

आप कैसे /कैसी/ हैं?
āp kaise /kaisī/ hain?

My name is ...

मेरा नाम ... है
mera nām ... hai.

His name is ...

इसका नाम ... है।
isaka nām ... hai.

Her name is ...

इसका नाम ... है।
isaka nām ... hai.

What's your name?

आपका क्या नाम है?
āpaka kya nām hai?

What's his name?

इसका क्या नाम है?
isaka kya nām hai?

What's her name?

इसका क्या नाम है?
isaka kya nām hai?

What's your last name?

आपका आख़िरी नाम क्या है?
āpaka ākhirī nām kya hai?

You can call me ...

आप मुझे ... बुला सकते /सकती/ हैं।
āp mujhe ... bula sakate /sakatī/ hain.

Where are you from?

आप कहाँ से हैं?
āp kahān se hain?

I'm from ...

मैं ... हूँ
main ... hūn.

What do you do for a living?

आप क्या काम करते /करती/ हैं?
āp kya kām karate /karatī/ hain?

Who is this?

यह कौन है?
yah kaun hai?

Who is he?

यह कौन है?
yah kaun hai?

Who is she?	यह कौन है?
	yah kaun hai?
Who are they?	ये कौन हैं?
	ye kaun hain?

This is ...	यह ... है
	yah ... hai.
my friend (masc.)	मेरा दोस्त
	mera dost
my friend (fem.)	मेरी सहेली
	merī sahelī
my husband	मेरे पति
	mere pati
my wife	मेरी पत्नी
	merī patnī

my father	मेरे पिता
	mere pita
my mother	मेरी माँ
	merī mān
my brother	मेरे भाई
	mere bhaī
my sister	मेरी बहन
	merī bahan
my son	मेरा बेटा
	mera beta
my daughter	मेरी बेटी
	merī betī

This is our son.	यह मेरा बेटा है
	yah mera beta hai.
This is our daughter.	यह मेरी बेटी है
	yah merī betī hai.
These are my children.	ये मेरे बच्चे हैं।
	ye mere bachche hain.
These are our children.	ये हमारे बच्चे हैं।
	ye hamāre bachche hain.

Farewells

Good bye!	अलविदा! alavida!
Bye! (inform.)	बाय! bāy!
See you tomorrow.	कल मिलते हैं kal milate hain.
See you soon.	जल्दी मिलते हैं। jaldī milate hain.
See you at seven.	सात बजे मिलते हैं। sāt baje milate hain.
Have fun!	मज़े करो! maze karo!
Talk to you later.	बाद में बात करते हैं। bād men bāt karate hain.
Have a nice weekend.	तुम्हारा समाहांत शुभ रहे tumhāra saptāhānt shubh rahe.
Good night.	शुभ रात्रि shubh rātri.
It's time for me to go.	मेरे जाने का वक्त हो गया है mere jāne ka vakt ho gaya hai.
I have to go.	मुझे जाना होगा। mujhe jāna hai.
I will be right back.	मैं अभी वापिस आता /आती/ हूँ main abhī vāpis āta /āṭī/ hūn.
It's late.	देर हो गई है। der ho gaī hai.
I have to get up early.	मुझे जल्दी उठना है। mujhe jaldī uthana hai.
I'm leaving tomorrow.	मैं कल जाने वाला /वाली/ हूँ main kal jāne vāla /vāṭī/ hūn.
We're leaving tomorrow.	हम कल जाने वाले हैं। ham kal jāne vāle hain.
Have a nice trip!	आपकी यात्रा शानदार हो! āpkī yātra shānadār ho!
It was nice meeting you.	आपसे मिलकर अच्छा लगा। āpase milakar achchha laga.
It was nice talking to you.	आपसे बातें करके अच्छा लगा। āpase bāten karake achchha laga.
Thanks for everything.	हर चीज़ के लिए शुक्रिया। har chīz ke lie shukriya.

I had a very good time.

मैंने बहुत अच्छा वक्त बिताया।
mainne bahut achchha vakt bitāya.

We had a very good time.

हमने बहुत अच्छा वक्त बिताया।
hamane bahut achchha vakt bitāya.

It was really great.

बहुत मज़ा आया।
bahut maza āya.

I'm going to miss you.

मुझे तुम्हारी याद आएगी।
mujhe tumhārī yād āegī.

We're going to miss you.

हमें आपकी याद आएगी।
hamen āpakī yād āegī.

Good luck!

गुड लक!
gud lak!

Say hi to ...

... को नमस्ते बोलना।
... ko namaste bolana.

Foreign language

I don't understand.	मुझे समझ नहीं आया।
	mujhe samajh nahin āya.
Write it down, please.	इसे लिख दीजिए, प्लीज़।
	ise likh dījie, plīz.
Do you speak ...?	क्या आप ... बोलते /बोलती/ हैं?
	kya āp ... bolate /bolatī/ hain?

I speak a little bit of ...	मैं थोड़ा-बहुत ... बोल सकता /सकती/ हूँ।
	main thora-bahut ... bol sakata /sakatī/ hūn.
English	अंग्रेज़ी
	angrezī

Turkish	तुर्की
	turkī
Arabic	अरबी
	arabī
French	फ्रांसिसी
	frānsisī

German	जर्मन
	jarman
Italian	इतालवी
	itālavī
Spanish	स्पेनी
	spenī

Portuguese	पुर्तगाली
	purtagālī
Chinese	चीनी
	chīnī
Japanese	जापानी
	jāpānī

Can you repeat that, please.	क्या आप इसे दोहरा सकते हैं
	kya āp ise dohara sakate hain.
I understand.	मैं समझ गया /गई/।
	main samajh gaya /gaī/.
I don't understand.	मुझे समझ नहीं आया।
	mujhe samajh nahin āya.
Please speak more slowly.	कृपया थोड़ा और धीरे बोलिये।
	kṛpaya thora aur dhīre boliye.

Is that correct? (Am I saying it right?)

क्या यह सही है?
kya yah sahī hai?

What is this? (What does this mean?)

यह क्या है?
yah kya hai?

Apologies

Excuse me, please.

मुझे माफ़ करना।
mujhe māf karana.

I'm sorry.

मुझे माफ़ कर दो।
mujhe māf karana.

I'm really sorry.

मैं बहुत शर्मिन्दा हूँ।
main bahut sharminda hūn.

Sorry, it's my fault.

माफ़ करना, यह मेरी गलती है।
māf karana, yah merī galatī hai.

My mistake.

मेरी गलती।
merī galatī.

May I ...?

क्या मैं ... सकता /सकती/ हूँ?
kya main ... sakata /sakatī/ hūn?

Do you mind if I ...?

क्या मैं ... सकता /सकती/ हूँ?
kya main ... sakata /sakatī/ hūn?

It's OK.

कोई बात नहीं।
koī bāt nahin.

It's all right.

सब कुछ ठीक है।
sab kuchh thīk hai.

Don't worry about it.

फिक्र मत करो।
fikr mat karo.

Agreement

Yes.
हाँ।
hān.

Yes, sure.
हाँ, बिल्कुल।
hān, bilkul.

OK (Good!)
ओके! बढ़िया!
oke! barhiya!

Very well.
ठीक है।
thīk hai.

Certainly!
बिल्कुल!
bilkul!

I agree.
मैं सहमत हूँ।
main sahamat hūn.

That's correct.
यह सही है।
yah sahī hai.

That's right.
यह ठीक है।
yah thīk hai.

You're right.
आप सही हैं।
āp sahī hain.

I don't mind.
मुझे बुरा नहीं लगेगा।
mujhe bura nahin lagega.

Absolutely right.
बिल्कुल सही।
bilkul sahī.

It's possible.
हो सकता है।
ho sakata hai.

That's a good idea.
यह अच्छा विचार है।
yah achchha vichār hai.

I can't say no.
मैं नहीं नहीं बोल सकता
/सकती/ हूँ।
main nahin nahin bol sakata
/sakatī/ hūn.

I'd be happy to.
मुझे ख़ुश होगी।
mujhe khush hogī.

With pleasure.
ख़ुशी से।
khushī se.

Refusal. Expressing doubt

No.	नहीं। nahin.
Certainly not.	बिल्कुल नहीं। bilkul nahin.
I don't agree.	मैं सहमत नहीं हूँ। main sahamat nahin hūn.
I don't think so.	मुझे नहीं लगता है। mujhe nahin lagata hai.
It's not true.	यह सही नहीं है। yah sahī nahin hai.
You are wrong.	आप गलत हैं। āp galat hain.
I think you are wrong.	मेरे ख्याल में आप गलत हैं। mere khyāl men āp galat hain.
I'm not sure.	मुझे पक्का नहीं पता है। mujhe pakka nahin pata hai.
It's impossible.	यह मुमकिन नहीं है। yah mumakin nahin hai.
Nothing of the kind (sort)!	ऐसा कुछ नहीं हुआ! aisa kuchh nahin hua!
The exact opposite.	इससे बिल्कुल उलटा। isase bilkul ulata.
I'm against it.	मैं इसके खिलाफ़ हूँ। main isake khilāf hūn.
I don't care.	मुझे कोई फर्क नहीं पड़ता। mujhe koī fark nahin parata.
I have no idea.	मुझे कुछ नहीं पता। mujhe kuchh nahin pata.
I doubt it.	मुझे इस बात पर शक है। mujhe is bāt par shak hai.
Sorry, I can't.	माफ़ करना, मैं नहीं कर सकता /सकती/ हूँ। māf karana, main nahin kar sakata /sakatī/ hūn.
Sorry, I don't want to.	माफ़ करना, मैं नहीं करना चाहता /चाहती/ हूँ। māf karana, main nahin karana chāhata /chāhatī/ hūn.
Thank you, but I don't need this.	शुक्रिया, मगर मुझे इसकी ज़रूरत नहीं है। shukriya, magar mujhe isakī zarūrat nahin hai.

It's getting late.

देर हो रही है।
der ho rahī hai.

I have to get up early.

मुझे जल्दी उठना है।
mujhe jaldī uthana hai.

I don't feel well.

मेरी तबियत ठीक नहीं है।
merī tabiyat thīk nahin hai.

Expressing gratitude

Thank you.

शुक्रिया।
shukriya.

Thank you very much.

बहुत बहुत शुक्रिया।
bahut bahut shukriya.

I really appreciate it.

मैं बहुत आभारी हूँ।
main bahut ābhārī hūn.

I'm really grateful to you.

मैं बहुत बहुत आभारी हूँ।
main bahut bahut ābhārī hūn.

We are really grateful to you.

हम बहुत आभारी हैं।
ham bahut ābhārī hain.

Thank you for your time.

आपके वक्त के लिए शुक्रिया।
āpake vakt ke lie shukriya.

Thanks for everything.

हर चीज़ के लिए शुक्रिया।
har chīz ke lie shukriya.

Thank you for ...

... के लिए शुक्रिया।
... ke lie shukriya.

your help

आपकी मदद
āpakī madad

a nice time

अच्छे वक्त
achchhe vakt

a wonderful meal

बढ़िया खाने
barhiya khāne

a pleasant evening

खुशनुमा शाम
khushanuma shām

a wonderful day

बढ़िया दिन
barhiya din

an amazing journey

अद्भुत सफर
adbhut safar

Don't mention it.

शुक्रिया की कोई ज़रूरत नहीं।
shukriya kī koī zarūrat nahin.

You are welcome.

आपका स्वागत है।
āpaka svāgat hai.

Any time.

कभी भी।
kabhī bhī.

My pleasure.

यह मेरे लिए खुशी की बात है।
yah mere lie khushī kī bāt hai.

Forget it.

भूल जाओ।
bhūl jao.

Don't worry about it.

फिक्र मत करो।
fikr mat karo.

Congratulations. Best wishes

Congratulations!
मुबारक हो!
mubārak ho!

Happy birthday!
जन्मदिन की बधाई!
janmadin kī badhaī!

Merry Christmas!
बड़ा दिन मुबारक हो!
bara din mubārak ho!

Happy New Year!
नए साल की बधाई!
nae sāl kī badhaī!

Happy Easter!
ईस्टर की शुभकामनाएं!
īstar kī shubhakāmanaen!

Happy Hanukkah!
हनुका की बधाईयाँ!
hanuka kī badhaīyān!

I'd like to propose a toast.
मैं एक टोस्ट करना चाहूँगा /चाहूँगी/।
main ek tost karana chāhūnga /chāhūngī/.

Cheers!
चियर्स!
chiyars!

Let's drink to …!
... के लिए पीया जाए!
... ke lie pīya jae!

To our success!
हमारी कामियाबी!
hamārī kāmiyābī!

To your success!
आपकी कामियाबी!
āpakī kāmiyābī!

Good luck!
गुड लक!
gud lak!

Have a nice day!
आपका दिन शुभ हो!
āpaka din shubh ho!

Have a good holiday!
आपकी छुट्टी अच्छी रहे!
āpakī chhuttī achchhī rahe!

Have a safe journey!
आपका सफर सुरक्षित रहे!
āpaka safar surakshit rahe!

I hope you get better soon!
मैं उम्मीद करता /करती/ हूँ कि आप जल्द ही ठीक हो जाएंगे!
main ummīd karata /karatī/ hūn ki āp jald hī thīk ho jaenge!

Socializing

Why are you sad?	आप उदास क्यों हैं? āp udās kyon hain?
Smile! Cheer up!	मुस्कुराओ! खुश रहो! muskurao! khush raho!
Are you free tonight?	क्या आप आज रात फ्री हैं? kya āp āj rāt frī hain?
May I offer you a drink?	क्या मैं आपके लिए एक ड्रिंक खरीद सकता /सकती/ हूँ? kya main āpake lie ek drink kharīd sakata /sakatī/ hūn?
Would you like to dance?	क्या आप डांस करना चाहेंगी /चाहेंगी/? kya āp dāns karana chāhengī /chāhengī/?
Let's go to the movies.	चलिए फ़िल्म देखने चलते हैं chalie film dekhane chalate hain.
May I invite you to ...?	क्या मैं आपको ... इन्वाइट कर सकता /सकती/ हूँ? kya main āpako ... invait kar sakata /sakatī/ hūn?
a restaurant	रेस्तरां restarān
the movies	फ़िल्म के लिए film ke lie
the theater	थियेटर के लिए thiyetar ke lie
go for a walk	वॉक के लिए vok ke lie
At what time?	कितने बजे? kitane baje?
tonight	आज रात āj rāt
at six	छह बजे chhah baje
at seven	सात बजे sāt baje
at eight	आठ बजे āth baje
at nine	नौ बजे nau baje

Do you like it here?	क्या आपको यहाँ अच्छा लगता है? kya āpako yahān achchha lagata hai?
Are you here with someone?	क्या आप यहाँ किसी के साथ आए /आई/ हैं? kya āp yahān kisī ke sāth āe /āī/ hain?
I'm with my friend.	मैं अपने दोस्त के साथ हूँ। main apane dost ke sāth hūn.
I'm with my friends.	मैं अपने दोस्तों के साथ हूँ। main apane doston ke sāth hūn.
No, I'm alone.	नहीं, मैं अकेला /अकेली/ हूँ। nahin, main akela /akelī/ hūn.
Do you have a boyfriend?	क्या आपका कोई बॉयफ्रेंड है? kya āpaka koī boyafrend hai?
I have a boyfriend.	मेरा बॉयफ्रेंड है। mera boyafrend hai.
Do you have a girlfriend?	क्या आपकी कोई गर्लफ्रेंड है? kya āpakī koī garlafrend hai?
I have a girlfriend.	मेरी एक गर्लफ्रेंड है। merī ek garlafrend hai.
Can I see you again?	क्या आपसे फिर मिल सकता /सकती/ हूँ? kya āpase fir mil sakata /sakatī/ hūn?
Can I call you?	क्या मैं आपको कॉल कर सकता /सकती/ हूँ? kya main āpako kol kar sakata /sakatī/ hūn?
Call me. (Give me a call.)	मुझे कॉल करना। mujhe kol karana.
What's your number?	आपका नंबर क्या है? āpaka nambar kya hai?
I miss you.	मुझे तुम्हारी याद आ रही है। mujhe tumhārī yād ā rahī hai.
You have a beautiful name.	आपका नाम बहुत खूबसूरत है। āpaka nām bahut khūbasūrat hai.
I love you.	मैं तुमसे प्यार करता /करती/ हूँ। main tumase pyār karata /karatī/ hūn.
Will you marry me?	क्या तुम मुझसे शादी करोगे /करोगी/? kya tum mujhase shādī karoge /karogī/?
You're kidding!	तुम मज़ाक कर रहे /रही/ हो! tum mazāk kar rahe /rahī/ ho!
I'm just kidding.	मैं बस मज़ाक कर रहा रही हूँ। main bas mazāk kar raha rahī hūn.
Are you serious?	क्या आप सीरियस हैं? kya āp sīriyas hain?
I'm serious.	मैं सीरियस हूँ। main sīriyas hūn.

Really?!	सच में?!
	sach men?!
It's unbelievable!	मुझे यकिन नहीं होता!
	mujhe yakin nahin hota!
I don't believe you.	मुझे तुम पर यकिन नहीं है।
	mujhe tum par yakin nahin hai.

I can't.	मैं नहीं आ सकता /सकती/।
	main nahin ā sakata /sakatī/.
I don't know.	मुझे नहीं मालूम।
	mujhe nahin mālūm.
I don't understand you.	मुझे आपकी बात समझ नहीं आई।
	mujhe āpakī bāt samajh nahin āī.
Please go away.	यहाँ से चले जाईये।
	yahān se chale jāīye.
Leave me alone!	मुझे अकेला छोड़ दो।
	mujhe akela chhor do!

I can't stand him.	मैं उसे बर्दाश्त नहीं कर सकता /सकती/ हूँ।
	main use bārdāsht nahin kar sakata /sakatī/ hūn.
You are disgusting!	तुमसे घिन्न आती है!
	tumase ghinn ātī hai!
I'll call the police!	मैं पुलिस बुला लूँगा /लूँगी/!
	main pulis bula lūnga /lūngī/!

Sharing impressions. Emotions

I like it. मुझे यह पसंद है।
mujhe yah pasand hai.

Very nice. बहुत अच्छा।
bahut achchha.

That's great! बहुत बढ़िया!
bahut barhiya!

It's not bad. बुरा नहीं है।
bura nahin hai.

I don't like it. मुझे यह पसंद नहीं है।
mujhe yah pasand nahin hai.

It's not good. यह अच्छा नहीं है।
yah achchha nahin hai.

It's bad. यह बुरा है।
yah bura hai.

It's very bad. यह बहुत बुरा है।
yah bahut bura hai.

It's disgusting. यह घिनौना है।
yah ghinauna hai.

I'm happy. मैं खुश हूँ।
main khush hūn.

I'm content. मैं संतुष्ट हूँ।
main santusht hūn.

I'm in love. मुझे प्यार हो गया है।
mujhe pyār ho gaya hai.

I'm calm. मैं शांत हूँ।
main shānt hūn.

I'm bored. मुझे बोरियत हो रही है।
mujhe boriyat ho rahī hai.

I'm tired. मैं थक गया /गई/ हूँ।
main thak gaya /gaī/ hūn.

I'm sad. मैं दुखी हूँ।
main dukhī hūn.

I'm frightened. मुझे डर लग रहा हैं।
mujhe dar lag raha hain.

I'm angry. मुझे गुस्सा आ रहा है।
mujhe gussa ā raha hai.

I'm worried. मैं परेशान हूँ।
main pareshān hūn.

I'm nervous. मुझे घवराहट हो रही है।
mujhe ghavarāhat ho rahī hai.

I'm jealous. (envious)

मुझे जलन हो रही है।
mujhe jalan ho rahī hai.

I'm surprised.

मुझे हैरानी हो रही है।
mujhe hairānī ho rahī hai.

I'm perplexed.

मुझे समझ नहीं आ रहा है।
mujhe samajh nahin ā raha hai.

Problems. Accidents

I've got a problem.	मुझे एक परेशानी है।
	mujhe ek pareshānī hai.
We've got a problem.	हमें परेशानी है।
	hamen pareshānī hai.
I'm lost.	मैं खो गया /गई/ हूँ।
	main kho gaya /gaī/ hūn.
I missed the last bus (train).	मुझसे आखिरी बस छूट गई।
	mujhase ākhirī bas chhūt gaī.
I don't have any money left.	मेरे पास पैसे नहीं बचे।
	mere pās paise nahin bache.

I've lost my …	मेरा … खो गया है।
	mera … kho gaya hai.
Someone stole my …	किसी ने मेरा … चुरा लिया।
	kisī ne mera … chura liya.
passport	पासपोर्ट
	pāsaport
wallet	बटुआ
	batua
papers	कागज़ात
	kāgazāt
ticket	टिकट
	tikat
money	पैसा
	paisa
handbag	पर्स
	pars
camera	कैमरा
	kaimara
laptop	लैपटॉप
	laipatop
tablet computer	टैबलेट
	taibalet
mobile phone	मोबाइल फ़ोन
	mobail fon

Help me!	मेरी मदद करो!
	merī madad karo!
What's happened?	क्या हुआ?
	kya hua?
fire	आग
	āg
shooting	गोलियाँ चल रही हैं
	goliyān chal rahī hain

murder	कत्ल हो गया है katl ho gaya hai
explosion	विस्फोट हो गया है visfot ho gaya hai
fight	लड़ाई हो गई है laraī ho gaī hai

Call the police!	पुलिस को बुलाओ! pulis ko bulāo!
Please hurry up!	कृपया जल्दी करें! kṛpaya jaldī karen!
I'm looking for the police station.	मैं पुलिस थाना ढूंढ रहा /रही/ हूँ. main pulis thāna dhūnrh raha /rahī/ hūn.
I need to make a call.	मुझे फ़ोन करना है. mujhe fon karana hai.
May I use your phone?	क्या मैं आपका फ़ोन इस्तेमाल कर सकता /सकती/ हूँ? kya main āpaka fon istemāl kar sakata /sakatī/ hūn?

mugged	मेरा सामान चुरा लिया गया है mera sāmān chura liya gaya hai
robbed	मुझे लूट लिया गया है mujhe lūt liya gaya hai
raped	मेरा बालात्कार किया गया है mera bālātkār kiya gaya hai
attacked (beaten up)	मुझे पीटा गया है mujhe pīta gaya hai

Are you all right?	क्या आप ठीक हैं? kya āp thīk hain?
Did you see who it was?	क्या आपने देखा कौन था? kya āpane dekha kaun tha?
Would you be able to recognize the person?	क्या आप उसे पहचान सकेंगे /सकेंगी/? kya āp use pahachān sakenge /sakengī/?
Are you sure?	क्या आपको यकीन है? kya āpako yakīn hai?

Please calm down.	कृपया शांत हो जाएं. kṛpaya shānt ho jaen.
Take it easy!	आराम से! ārām se!
Don't worry!	चिंता मत करो! chinta mat karo!
Everything will be fine.	सब ठीक हो जायेगा. sab thīk ho jāyega.
Everything's all right.	सब कुछ ठीक है. sab kuchh thīk hai.
Come here, please.	कृपया यहाँ आइये. kṛpaya yahān āiye.

I have some questions for you.

मेरे पास तुम्हारे लिए कुछ प्रश्न है।
mere pās tumhāre lie kuchh prashn hai.

Wait a moment, please.

कृपया एक क्षण रुकें।
kr̥paya ek kshan ruken.

Do you have any I.D.?

क्या आपके पास आईडी है?
kya āpake pās āīdī hai?

Thanks. You can leave now.

धन्यवाद। आप अब जा सकते
/सकती/ है।
dhanyavād. āp ab ja sakate
/sakatī/ hain.

Hands behind your head!

अपने हाथ सिर के पीछे रखें!
apane hāth sir ke pīchhe rakhen!

You're under arrest!

आप हिरासत में हैं!
āp hirāsat men hain!

Health problems

Please help me.	कृपया मेरी मदद करें। krpaya merī madad karen.
I don't feel well.	मेरी तबियत ठीक नहीं है। merī tabiyat thīk nahin hai.
My husband doesn't feel well.	मेरे पति को ठीक महसूस नहीं हो रहा है। mere pati ko thīk mahasūs nahin ho raha hai.
My son …	मेरे बेटे … mere bete …
My father …	मेरे पिता … mere pita …
My wife doesn't feel well.	मेरी पत्नी को ठीक महसूस नहीं हो रहा है। merī patnī ko thīk mahasūs nahin ho raha hai.
My daughter …	मेरी बेटी … merī betī …
My mother …	मेरी माँ … merī mãn …
headache	मुझे सिरदर्द है। mujhe siradard hai.
sore throat	मेरा गला ख़राब है। mera gala kharāb hai.
stomach ache	मेरे पेट में दर्द है। mere pet men dard hai.
toothache	मेरे दाँत में दर्द है। mere dãnt men dard hai.
I feel dizzy.	मुझे चक्कर आ रहा है। mujhe chakkar ā raha hai.
He has a fever.	इसे बुख़ार है। ise bukhār hai.
She has a fever.	इसे बुख़ार है। ise bukhār hai.
I can't breathe.	मैं साँस नहीं ले पा रहा /रही/ हूँ। main sāns nahin le pa raha /rahī/ hūn.
I'm short of breath.	मेरी साँस फूल रही है। merī sāns fūl rahī hai.
I am asthmatic.	मुझे दमा है। mujhe dama hai.

I am diabetic.	मैं मधुमेह का /की/ रोगी हूँ। main madhumeh ka /kī/ rogī hūn.
I can't sleep.	मैं सो नहीं पा रहा /रही/ हूँ। main so nahin pa raha /rahī/ hūn.
food poisoning	फ़ूड पॉपज़निंग fūd poezaning

It hurts here.	यहाँ दुखता हैं। yahān dukhata hain.
Help me!	मेरी मदद करो! merī madad karo!
I am here!	मैं यहाँ हूँ! main yahān hūn!
We are here!	हम यहाँ हैं! ham yahān hain!
Get me out of here!	मुझे यहां से बाहर निकालो! mujhe yahān se bāhar nikālo!

I need a doctor.	मुझे एक डॉक्टर की ज़रुरत है। mujhe ek doktar kī zarurat hai.
I can't move.	मैं हिल नहीं सकता /सकती/ हूँ। main hil nahin sakata /sakatī/ hūn.
I can't move my legs.	मैं अपने पैरों को नहीं हिला पा रहा /रही/ हूँ। main apane pairon ko nahin hila pa raha /rahī/ hūn.

I have a wound.	मुझे चोट लगी है। mujhe chot lagī hai.
Is it serious?	क्या यह गंभीर है? kya yah gambhīr hai?
My documents are in my pocket.	मेरे दस्तावेज़ मेरी जेब में हैं। mere dastāvez merī jeb men hain.
Calm down!	शांत हो जाओ! shānt ho jao!
May I use your phone?	क्या मैं आपका फ़ोन इस्तेमाल कर सकता /सकती/ हूँ? kya main āpaka fon istemāl kar sakata /sakatī/ hūn?

Call an ambulance!	एम्बुलेन्स बुलाओ! embulens bulao!
It's urgent!	बहुत ज़रूरी है। bahut zarūrī hai!
It's an emergency!	यह एक आपातकाल है। yah ek āpātakāl hai!
Please hurry up!	कृपया जल्दी करें। kṛpaya jaldī karen!
Would you please call a doctor?	क्या आप डॉक्टर को बुला देंगे /देंगी/? kya āp doktar ko bula denge /dengī/?
Where is the hospital?	अस्पताल कहाँ है? aspatāl kahān hai?

How are you feeling? आप कैसा महसूस कर रहे /रही/ हैं?
āp kaisa mahasūs kar rahe /rahī/ hain?

Are you all right? क्या आप ठीक हैं?
kya āp thīk hain?

What's happened? क्या हुआ?
kya hūa?

I feel better now. मैं अब ठीक हूँ।
main ab thīk hūn.

It's OK. सब ठीक है।
sab thīk hai.

It's all right. सब कुछ ठीक है।
sab kuchh thīk hai.

At the pharmacy

pharmacy (drugstore)	दवा की दुकान dava kī dukān
24-hour pharmacy	चौबीस घंटे खुलने वाली दवा की दुकान chaubīs ghante khulane vālī dava kī dukān
Where is the closest pharmacy?	सबसे करीबी दवा की दुकान कहाँ है? sabase karībī dava kī dukān kahān hai?
Is it open now?	क्या वह अभी खुली है? kya vah abhī khulī hai?
At what time does it open?	वह कितने बजे खुलती है? vah kitane baje khulatī hai?
At what time does it close?	वह कितने बजे बंद होती है? vah kitane baje band hotī hai?
Is it far?	क्या वह दूर है? kya vah dūr hai?
Can I get there on foot?	क्या मैं वहाँ पैदल जा सकता /सकती/ हूँ? kya main vahān paidal ja sakata /sakatī/ hūn?
Can you show me on the map?	क्या आप मुझे नक्शे पर दिखा सकते /सकती/ हैं? kya āp mujhe nakshe par dikha sakate /sakatī/ hain?
Please give me something for ...	मुझे ... के लिए कुछ दे दें। mujhe ... ke lie kuchh de den.
a headache	सिरदर्द siradard
a cough	खाँसी khānsī
a cold	जुकाम zukām
the flu	जुकाम-बुखार zukām-bukhār
a fever	बुखार bukhār
a stomach ache	पेट दर्द pet dard
nausea	मतली matalī

diarrhea	दस्त
	dast
constipation	कब्ज
	kabz

pain in the back	पीठ दर्द
	pīth dard
chest pain	सीने में दर्द
	sīne men dard
side stitch	पेट की माँसपेशी में दर्द
	pet kī mānsapeshī men dard
abdominal pain	पेट दर्द
	pet dard

pill	दवा
	dava
ointment, cream	मरहम, क्रीम
	maraham, krīm
syrup	सिरप
	sirap
spray	स्प्रे
	spre
drops	ड्रॉप
	drop

You need to go to the hospital.	आपको अस्पताल जाना चाहिए।
	āpako aspatāl jāna chāhie.
health insurance	स्वास्थ्य बीमा
	svāsthy bīma
prescription	नुस्खा
	nuskha
insect repellant	कीटरोधक
	kītarodhak
Band Aid	बैंड एड
	baind ed

The bare minimum

Excuse me, ...	माफ़ कीजिएगा, ... māf kījiega, ...
Hello.	नमस्कार। namaskār.
Thank you.	शुक्रिया। shukriya.
Good bye.	अलविदा। alavida.
Yes.	हाँ। hān.
No.	नहीं। nahin.
I don't know.	मुझे नहीं मालूम। mujhe nahin mālūm.
Where? | Where to? | When?	कहाँ? | कहाँ जाना है? | कब? kahān? | kahān jāna hai? | kab?
I need ...	मुझे ... चाहिए। mujhe ... chāhie.
I want ...	मैं ... चाहता /चाहती/ हूँ। main ... chāhata /chāhatī/ hūn.
Do you have ...?	क्या आपके पास ... है? kya āpake pās ... hai?
Is there a ... here?	क्या यहाँ ... है? kya yahān ... hai?
May I ...?	क्या मैं ... सकता /सकती/ हूँ? kya main ... sakata /sakatī/ hūn?
..., please (polite request)	..., कृपया। ..., krpaya.
I'm looking for ...	मैं ... ढूंढ रहा /रही/ हूँ। main ... dhūnrh raha /rahī/ hūn.
restroom	शौचालय shauchālay
ATM	एटीएम etīem
pharmacy (drugstore)	दवा की दुकान dava kī dukān
hospital	अस्पताल aspatāl
police station	पुलिस थाना pulis thāna
subway	मेट्रो metro

taxi	टैक्सी taiksī
train station	ट्रेन स्टेशन tren steshan

My name is ...	मेरा नाम ... है। mera nām ... hai
What's your name?	आपका क्या नाम है? āpaka kya nām hai?
Could you please help me?	क्या आप मेरी मदद कर सकते /सकती/ हैं? kya āp merī madad kar sakate /sakatī/ hain?
I've got a problem.	मुझे एक परेशानी है। mujhe ek pareshānī hai.
I don't feel well.	मेरी तबियत ठीक नहीं है। merī tabiyat thīk nahin hai.
Call an ambulance!	एम्बुलेन्स बुलाओ! embulens bulao!
May I make a call?	क्या मैं एक फ़ोन कर सकता /सकती/ हूँ? kya main ek fon kar sakata /sakatī/ hūn?

I'm sorry.	मुझे माफ़ करना। mujhe māf kar do.
You're welcome.	आपका स्वागत है। āpaka svāgat hai.

I, me	मैं main
you (inform.)	तू tū
he	वह vah
she	वह vah
they (masc.)	वे ve
they (fem.)	वे ve
we	हम ham
you (pl)	तुम tum
you (sg, form.)	आप āp

ENTRANCE	प्रवेश pravesh
EXIT	निकास nikās

OUT OF ORDER	ख़राब है kharāb hai
CLOSED	बंद band
OPEN	खुला khula
FOR WOMEN	महिलाओं के लिए mahilaon ke lie
FOR MEN	पुरूषों के लिए purūshon ke lie

CONCISE DICTIONARY

This section contains more than 1,500 useful words arranged alphabetically. The dictionary includes a lot of gastronomic terms and will be helpful when ordering food at a restaurant or buying groceries

T&P Books Publishing

DICTIONARY CONTENTS

1. Time. Calendar	78
2. Numbers. Numerals	79
3. Humans. Family	80
4. Human body	81
5. Medicine. Diseases. Drugs	83
6. Feelings. Emotions. Conversation	84
7. Clothing. Personal accessories	85
8. City. Urban institutions	86
9. Money. Finances	88
10. Transportation	89
11. Food. Part 1	90
12. Food. Part 2	91
13. House. Apartment. Part 1	92
14. House. Apartment. Part 2	94
15. Professions. Social status	95
16. Sport	96

T&P Books Publishing

17. Foreign languages. Orthography	97
18. The Earth. Geography	99
19. Countries of the world. Part 1	100
20. Countries of the world. Part 2	101
21. Weather. Natural disasters	102
22. Animals. Part 1	104
23. Animals. Part 2	105
24. Trees. Plants	106
25. Various useful words	107
26. Modifiers. Adjectives. Part 1	109
27. Modifiers. Adjectives. Part 2	110
28. Verbs. Part 1	111
29. Verbs. Part 2	112
30. Verbs. Part 3	113

T&P Books Publishing

time	वक़्त (m)	vakt
hour	घंटा (m)	ghanta
half an hour	आधा घंटा	ādha ghanta
minute	मिनट (m)	minat
second	सेकन्ड (m)	sekand
today (adv)	आज	āj
tomorrow (adv)	कल	kal
yesterday (adv)	कल	kal
Monday	सोमवार (m)	somavār
Tuesday	मंगलवार (m)	mangalavār
Wednesday	बुधवार (m)	budhavār
Thursday	गुरूवार (m)	gurūvār
Friday	शुक्रवार (m)	shukravār
Saturday	शनिवार (m)	shanivār
Sunday	रविवार (m)	ravivār
day	दिन (m)	din
working day	कार्यदिवस (m)	kāryadivas
public holiday	सार्वजनिक छुट्टी (f)	sārvajanik chhuttī
weekend	सप्ताहांत (m)	saptāhānt
week	हफ़ता (f)	hafata
last week (adv)	पिछले हफ़ते	pichhale hafate
next week (adv)	अगले हफ़ते	agale hafate
sunrise	सूर्योदय (m)	sūryoday
sunset	सूर्यास्त (m)	sūryāst
in the morning	सुबह में	subah men
in the afternoon	दोपहर में	dopahar men
in the evening	शाम में	shām men
tonight (this evening)	आज शाम	āj shām
at night	रात में	rāt men
midnight	आधी रात (f)	ādhī rāt
January	जनवरी (m)	janavarī
February	फ़रवरी (m)	faravarī
March	मार्च (m)	mārch
April	अप्रैल (m)	aprail
May	माई (m)	maī
June	जून (m)	jūn

July	जुलाई (m)	julaī
August	अगस्त (m)	agast
September	सितम्बर (m)	sitambar
October	अक्तूबर (m)	aktūbar
November	नवम्बर (m)	navambar
December	दिसम्बर (m)	disambar

in spring	वसन्त में	vasant men
in summer	गरमियों में	garamiyon men
in fall	शरद में	sharad men
in winter	सर्दियों में	sardiyon men

month	महीना (m)	mahīna
season (summer, etc.)	मौसम (m)	mausam
year	वर्ष (m)	varsh
century	शताबदी (f)	shatābadī

2. Numbers. Numerals

digit, figure	अंक (m)	ank
number	संख्या (f)	sankhya
minus sign	घटाव चिह्न (m)	ghatāv chihn
plus sign	जोड़ चिह्न (m)	jor chihn
sum, total	कुल (m)	kul

first (adj)	पहला	pahala
second (adj)	दूसरा	dūsara
third (adj)	तीसरा	tīsara

0 zero	ज़ीरो	zīro
1 one	एक	ek
2 two	दो	do
3 three	तीन	tīn
4 four	चार	chār

5 five	पाँच	pānch
6 six	छह	chhah
7 seven	सात	sāt
8 eight	आठ	āth
9 nine	नौ	nau
10 ten	दस	das

11 eleven	ग्यारह	gyārah
12 twelve	बारह	bārah
13 thirteen	तेरह	terah
14 fourteen	चौदह	chaudah
15 fifteen	पन्द्रह	pandrah

| 16 sixteen | सोलह | solah |
| 17 seventeen | सत्रह | satrah |

18 eighteen	अठारह	athārah
19 nineteen	उन्नीस	unnīs
20 twenty	बीस	bīs
30 thirty	तीस	tīs
40 forty	चालीस	chālīs
50 fifty	पचास	pachās
60 sixty	साठ	sāth
70 seventy	सत्तर	sattar
80 eighty	अस्सी	assī
90 ninety	नब्बे	nabbe
100 one hundred	सौ	sau
200 two hundred	दो सौ	do sau
300 three hundred	तीन सौ	tīn sau
400 four hundred	चार सौ	chār sau
500 five hundred	पाँच सौ	pānch sau
600 six hundred	छह सौ	chhah sau
700 seven hundred	सात सो	sāt so
800 eight hundred	आठ सौ	āth sau
900 nine hundred	नौ सौ	nau sau
1000 one thousand	एक हज़ार	ek hazār
10000 ten thousand	दस हज़ार	das hazār
one hundred thousand	एक लाख	ek lākh
million	दस लाख (m)	das lākh
billion	अरब (m)	arab

3. Humans. Family

man (adult male)	आदमी (m)	ādamī
young man	युवक (m)	yuvak
teenager	किशोर (m)	kishor
woman	औरत (f)	aurat
girl (young woman)	लड़की (f)	larakī
age	उम्र (f)	umr
adult (adj)	व्यस्क	vyask
middle-aged (adj)	अधेड़	adhed
elderly (adj)	बुजुर्ग	buzurg
old (adj)	साल	sāl
old man	बूढ़ा आदमी (m)	būrha ādamī
old woman	बूढ़ी औरत (f)	būrhī aurat
retirement	सेवा-निवृति (f)	seva-nivrtti
to retire (from job)	सेवा-निवृत्त होना	seva-nivrtt hona
retiree	सेवा-निवृत्त (m)	seva-nivrtt

mother	माँ (f)	mān
father	पिता (m)	pita
son	बेटा (m)	beta
daughter	बेटी (f)	betī
brother	भाई (m)	bhaī
sister	बहन (f)	bahan

parents	माँ-बाप (m pl)	mān-bāp
child	बच्चा (m)	bachcha
children	बच्चे (m pl)	bachche
stepmother	सौतेली माँ (f)	sautelī mān
stepfather	सौतेले पिता (m)	sautele pita

grandmother	दादी (f)	dādī
grandfather	दादा (m)	dāda
grandson	पोता (m)	pota
granddaughter	पोती (f)	potī
grandchildren	पोते (m)	pote

uncle	चाचा (m)	chācha
aunt	चाची (f)	chāchī
nephew	भतीजा (m)	bhatīja
niece	भतीजी (f)	bhatījī

wife	पत्नी (f)	patnī
husband	पति (m)	pati
married (masc.)	शादीशुदा	shādīshuda
married (fem.)	शादीशुदा	shādīshuda
widow	विधवा (f)	vidhava
widower	विधुर (m)	vidhur

| name (first name) | पहला नाम (m) | pahala nām |
| surname (last name) | उपनाम (m) | upanām |

relative	रिश्तेदार (m)	rishtedār
friend (masc.)	दोस्त (m)	dost
friendship	दोस्ती (f)	dostī

partner	पार्टनर (m)	pārtanar
superior (n)	अधीक्षक (m)	adhīkshak
colleague	सहकर्मी (m)	sahakarmī
neighbors	पड़ोसी (m pl)	parosī

4. Human body

organism (body)	शरीर (m)	sharīr
body	शरीर (m)	sharīr
heart	दिल (m)	dil
blood	खून (f)	khūn
brain	मस्तिष्क (m)	māstishk

nerve	नस (f)	nas
bone	हड्डी (f)	haddī
skeleton	कंकाल (m)	kankāl
spine (backbone)	रीढ़ की हड्डी	rīrh kī haddī
rib	पसली (f)	pasalī
skull	खोपड़ी (f)	khoparī

muscle	मांसपेशी (f)	mānsapeshī
lungs	फेफड़े (m pl)	fefare
skin	त्वचा (f)	tvacha

head	सिर (m)	sir
face	चेहरा (m)	chehara
nose	नाक (f)	nāk
forehead	माथा (m)	mātha
cheek	गाल (m)	gāl

mouth	मुँह (m)	munh
tongue	जीभ (m)	jībh
tooth	दाँत (f)	dānt
lips	होंठ (m)	honth
chin	ठोड़ी (f)	thorī

ear	कान (m)	kān
neck	गरदन (m)	garadan
throat	गला (m)	gala

eye	आँख (f)	ānkh
pupil	आँख की पुतली (f)	ānkh kī putalī
eyebrow	भौंह (f)	bhaunh
eyelash	बरौनी (f)	baraunī

hair	बाल (m pl)	bāl
hairstyle	हेयरस्टाइल (m)	heyarastail
mustache	मूँछें (f pl)	mūnchhen
beard	दाढ़ी (f)	dārhī
to have (a beard, etc.)	होना	hona
bald (adj)	गंजा	ganja

hand	हाथ (m)	hāth
arm	बाँह (m)	bānh
finger	उँगली (m)	ungalī
nail	नाखून (m)	nākhūn
palm	हथेली (f)	hathelī

shoulder	कंधा (m)	kandha
leg	टाँग (f)	tāng
foot	पैर का तलवा (m)	pair ka talava
knee	घुटना (m)	ghutana
heel	एड़ी (f)	erī
back	पीठ (f)	pīth
waist	कमर (f)	kamar

beauty mark	सौंदर्य चिन्ह (f)	saundary chinh
birthmark	जन्म चिह्न (m)	janm chihn
(café au lait spot)		

5. Medicine. Diseases. Drugs

health	सेहत (f)	sehat
well (not sick)	तंदरूस्त	tandarūst
sickness	बीमारी (f)	bīmārī
to be sick	बीमार होना	bīmār hona
ill, sick (adj)	बीमार	bīmār

cold (illness)	ज़ुकाम (f)	zukām
to catch a cold	ज़ुकाम हो जाना	zukām ho jāna
tonsillitis	टॉन्सिल (m)	tonsil
pneumonia	निमोनिया (f)	nimoniya
flu, influenza	फ़्लू (m)	flū

runny nose (coryza)	नज़ला (m)	nazala
cough	खाँसी (f)	khānsī
to cough (vi)	खाँसना	khānsana
to sneeze (vi)	छींकना	chhīnkana

stroke	स्ट्रोक (m)	strok
heart attack	दिल का दौरा (m)	dil ka daura
allergy	एलर्जी (f)	elarjī
asthma	दमा (f)	dama
diabetes	शूगर (f)	shūgar

tumor	ट्यूमर (m)	tyūmar
cancer	कर्क रोग (m)	kark rog
alcoholism	शराबीपन (m)	sharābīpan
AIDS	ऐइस (m)	aids
fever	बुख़ार (m)	bukhār
seasickness	जहाज़ी मतली (f)	jahāzī matalī

bruise (hématome)	नील (m)	nīl
bump (lump)	गुमड़ा (m)	gumara
to limp (vi)	लंगड़ाना	langarāna
dislocation	हड्डी खिसकना (f)	haddī khisakana
to dislocate (vt)	हड्डी खिसकना	haddī khisakana

fracture	हड्डी टूट जाना (f)	haddī tūt jāna
burn (injury)	जला होना	jala hona
injury	चोट (f)	chot
pain, ache	दर्द (f)	dard
toothache	दाँत दर्द (m)	dānt dard

| to sweat (perspire) | पसीना निकलना | pasīna nikalana |
| deaf (adj) | बहरा | bahara |

mute (adj)	गूँगा	gūnga
immunity	रोग प्रतिरोधक शक्ति (f)	rog pratirodhak shakti
virus	विषाणु (m)	vishānu
microbe	कीटाणु (m)	kītānu
bacterium	जीवाणु (m)	jīvānu
infection	संक्रमण (m)	sankraman

hospital	अस्पताल (m)	aspatāl
cure	इलाज (m)	ilāj
to vaccinate (vt)	टीका लगाना	tīka lagāna
to be in a coma	कोमा में चले जाना	koma men chale jāna
intensive care	गहन चिकित्सा (f)	gahan chikitsa
symptom	लक्षण (m)	lakshan
pulse	नब्ज़ (f)	nabz

6. Feelings. Emotions. Conversation

I, me	मैं	main
you	तुम	tum
he, she, it	वह	vah

we	हम	ham
you (to a group)	आप	āp
they	वे	ve
Hello! (fam.)	नमस्कार!	namaskār!
Hello! (form.)	नमस्ते!	namaste!
Good morning!	नमस्ते!	namaste!
Good afternoon!	नमस्ते!	namaste!
Good evening!	नमस्ते!	namaste!

to say hello	नमस्कार कहना	namaskār kahana
to greet (vt)	अभिवादन करना	abhivādan karana
How are you?	आप कैसे हैं?	āp kaise hain?
Bye-Bye! Goodbye!	अलविदा!	alavida!
Thank you!	धन्यवाद!	dhanyavād!

feelings	भावनाएं (f)	bhāvanaen
to be hungry	भूख लगना	bhūkh lagana
to be thirsty	प्यास लगना	pyās lagana
tired (adj)	थका हुआ	thaka hua

to be worried	फ़िक्रमंद होना	fikramand hona
to be nervous	घबराना	ghabarāna
hope	आशा (f)	āsha
to hope (vi, vt)	आशा रखना	āsha rakhana

character	चरित्र (m)	charitr
modest (adj)	विनम्र	vinamr
lazy (adj)	आलसी	ālasī
generous (adj)	उदार	udār

talented (adj)	प्रतिभाशाली	pratibhāshālī
honest (adj)	ईमानदार	īmānadār
serious (adj)	गम्भीर	gambhīr
shy, timid (adj)	शर्मीला	sharmīla
sincere (adj)	हार्दिक	hārdik
coward	कायर (m)	kāyar

to sleep (vi)	सोना	sona
dream	सपना (f)	sapana
bed	पलंग (m)	palang
pillow	तकिया (m)	takiya

insomnia	अनिद्रा (m)	anidra
to go to bed	सोने जाना	sone jāna
nightmare	डरावना सपना (m)	darāvana sapana
alarm clock	अलार्म घड़ी (f)	alārm gharī

smile	मुस्कान (f)	muskān
to smile (vi)	मुस्कुराना	muskurāna
to laugh (vi)	हंसना	hansana

quarrel	झगड़ा (m)	jhagara
insult	अपमान (m)	apamān
resentment	द्वेष (f)	dvesh
angry (mad)	नाराज़	nārāz

7. Clothing. Personal accessories

clothes	कपड़े (m)	kapare
coat (overcoat)	ओवरकोट (m)	ovarakot
fur coat	फरकोट (m)	farakot
jacket (e.g., leather ~)	जैकेट (f)	jaiket
raincoat (trenchcoat, etc.)	बरसाती (f)	barasātī

shirt (button shirt)	कमीज़ (f)	kamīz
pants	पैंट (m)	paint
suit jacket	कोट (m)	kot
suit	सूट (m)	sūt

dress (frock)	फ्रॉक (f)	frok
skirt	स्कर्ट (f)	skart
T-shirt	टी-शर्ट (f)	tī-shart
bathrobe	बाथ रोब (m)	bāth rob
pajamas	पज़ामा (m)	pajāma
workwear	वर्दी (f)	vardī

underwear	अंगवस्त्र (m)	angavastr
socks	मोज़े (m pl)	moze
bra	ब्रा (f)	bra
pantyhose	टाइट्स (m pl)	taits

stockings (thigh highs)	स्टाकिंग (m pl)	stāking
bathing suit	स्विम सूट (m)	svim sūt
hat	टोपी (f)	topī
footwear	पनही (f)	panahī
boots (e.g., cowboy ~)	बूट (m pl)	būt
heel	एड़ी (f)	erī
shoestring	जूते का फ़ीता (m)	jūte ka fīta
shoe polish	बूट-पालिश (m)	būt-pālish
cotton (n)	कपास (m)	kapās
wool (n)	ऊन (m)	ūn
fur (n)	फ़र (m)	far
gloves	दस्ताने (m pl)	dastāne
mittens	दस्ताने (m pl)	dastāne
scarf (muffler)	मफ़लर (m)	mafalar
glasses (eyeglasses)	ऐनक (m pl)	ainak
umbrella	छतरी (f)	chhatarī
tie (necktie)	टाई (f)	taī
handkerchief	रूमाल (m)	rūmāl
comb	कंघा (m)	kangha
hairbrush	ब्रश (m)	brash
buckle	बकसुआ (m)	bakasua
belt	बेल्ट (m)	belt
purse	पर्स (m)	pars
collar	कॉलर (m)	kolar
pocket	जेब (m)	jeb
sleeve	आस्तीन (f)	āstīn
fly (on trousers)	ज़िप (f)	zip
zipper (fastener)	ज़िप (f)	zip
button	बटन (m)	batan
to get dirty (vi)	मैला होना	maila hona
stain (mark, spot)	धब्बा (m)	dhabba

8. City. Urban institutions

store	दुकान (f)	dukān
shopping mall	शॉपिंग मॉल (m)	shoping mol
supermarket	सुपर बाज़ार (m)	supar bāzār
shoe store	जूते की दुकान (f)	jūte kī dukān
bookstore	किताबों की दुकान (f)	kitābon kī dukān
drugstore, pharmacy	दवाख़ाना (m)	davākhāna
bakery	बेकरी (f)	bekarī
pastry shop	टॉफ़ी की दुकान (f)	tofī kī dukān

grocery store	परचून की दुकान (f)	parachūn kī dukān
butcher shop	गोश्त की दुकान (f)	gosht kī dukān
produce store	सब्ज़ियों की दुकान (f)	sabziyon kī dukān
market	बाज़ार (m)	bāzār
hair salon	नाई की दुकान (f)	naī kī dukān
post office	डाकघर (m)	dākaghar
dry cleaners	ड्राइक्लीनर (m)	draiklīnar
circus	सर्कस (m)	sarkas
zoo	चिड़ियाघर (m)	chiriyāghar
theater	रंगमंच (m)	rangamanch
movie theater	सिनेमाघर (m)	sinemāghar
museum	संग्रहालय (m)	sangrahālay
library	पुस्तकालय (m)	pustakālay
mosque	मस्जिद (m)	masjid
synagogue	सीनागोग (m)	sīnāgog
cathedral	गिरजाघर (m)	girajāghar
temple	मंदिर (m)	mandir
church	गिरजाघर (m)	girajāghar
college	कॉलेज (m)	kolej
university	विश्वविद्यालय (m)	vishvavidyālay
school	विद्यालय (m)	vidyālay
hotel	होटल (f)	hotal
bank	बैंक (m)	baink
embassy	दूतावस (m)	dūtāvas
travel agency	पर्यटन आफ़िस (m)	paryatan āfis
subway	मेट्रो (m)	metro
hospital	अस्पताल (m)	aspatāl
gas station	पेट्रोल पम्प (f)	petrol pamp
parking lot	पार्किंग (f)	pārking
ENTRANCE	प्रवेश	pravesh
EXIT	निकास	nikās
PUSH	धक्का दें	dhakka den
PULL	खींचे	khīnche
OPEN	खुला	khula
CLOSED	बंद	band
monument	स्मारक (m)	smārak
fortress	किला (m)	kila
palace	भवन (m)	bhavan
medieval (adj)	मध्ययुगीय	madhayayugīy
ancient (adj)	प्राचीन	prāchīn
national (adj)	राष्ट्रीय	rāshtrīy
famous (monument, etc.)	मशहूर	mashhūr

9. Money. Finances

money	पैसा (m pl)	paisa
coin	सिक्का (m)	sikka
dollar	डॉलर (m)	dolar
euro	यूरो (m)	yūro
ATM	एटीएम (m)	etīem
currency exchange	मुद्रालय (m)	mudrālay
exchange rate	विनिमय दर (m)	vinimay dar
cash	कैश (m pl)	kaish
How much?	कितना?	kitana?
to pay (vi, vt)	दाम चुकाना	dām chukāna
payment	भुगतान (m)	bhugatān
change (give the ~)	चिल्लर (m)	chillar
price	दाम (m)	dām
discount	डिस्काउन्ट (m)	diskaunt
cheap (adj)	सस्ता	sasta
expensive (adj)	महंगा	mahanga
bank	बैंक (m)	baink
account	बैंक खाता (m)	baink khāta
credit card	क्रेडिट कार्ड (m)	kredit kārd
check	चेक (m)	chek
to write a check	चेक लिखना	chek likhana
checkbook	चेकबुक (f)	chekabuk
debt	कर्ज़ (m)	karz
debtor	क़र्ज़दार (m)	qarzadār
to lend (money)	कर्ज़ देना	karz dena
to borrow (vi, vt)	कर्ज़ लेना	karz lena
to rent (~ a tuxedo)	किराए पर लेना	kirae par lena
on credit (adv)	क्रेडिट पर	kredit par
wallet	बटुआ (m)	batua
safe	लॉकर (m)	lokar
inheritance	उत्तराधिकार (m)	uttarādhikār
fortune (wealth)	संपत्ति (f)	sampatti
tax	टैक्स (m)	taiks
fine	जुर्माना (m)	jurmāna
to fine (vt)	जुर्माना लगाना	jurmāna lagāna
wholesale (adj)	थोक	thok
retail (adj)	खुदरा	khudara
to insure (vt)	बीमा करना	bīma karana
insurance	बीमा (m)	bīma
capital	पूँजी (f)	pūnjī
turnover	कुल बिक्री (f)	kul bikrī

stock (share)	शेयर (f)	sheyar
profit	नफ़ा (m)	nafa
profitable (adj)	लाभदायक	lābhadāyak

crisis	संकट (m)	sankat
bankruptcy	दिवाला (m)	divāla
to go bankrupt	दिवालिया हो जाना	divāliya ho jāna

accountant	लेखापाल (m)	lekhāpāl
salary	आय (f)	āy
bonus (money)	बोनस (m)	bonas

10. Transportation

bus	बस (f)	bas
streetcar	ट्रैम (m)	traim
trolley bus	ट्रॉलीबस (f)	trolības

to go by ...	के माध्यम से जाना	ke mādhyam se jāna
to get on (~ the bus)	सवार होना	savār hona
to get off ...	उतरना	utarana

stop (e.g., bus ~)	बस स्टॉप (m)	bas stop
terminus	अंतिम स्टेशन (m)	antim steshan
schedule	समय सारणी (f)	samay sāranī
ticket	टिकट (m)	tikat
to be late (for ...)	देर हो जाना	der ho jāna

taxi, cab	टैक्सी (m)	taiksī
by taxi	टैक्सी से (m)	taiksī se
taxi stand	टैक्सी स्टैंड (m)	taiksī staind

traffic	यातायात (f)	yātāyāt
rush hour	भीड़ का समय (m)	bhīr ka samay
to park (vi)	पार्क करना	pārk karana

subway	मेट्रो (m)	metro
station	स्टेशन (m)	steshan
train	रेलगाड़ी, ट्रेन (f)	relagārī, tren
train station	स्टेशन (m)	steshan
rails	पटरियाँ (f)	patariyān
compartment	डिब्बा (m)	dibba
berth	बर्थ (f)	barth

airplane	विमान (m)	vimān
air ticket	हवाई टिकट (m)	havaī tikat
airline	हवाई कम्पनी (f)	havaī kampanī
airport	हवाई अड्डा (m)	havaī adda
flight (act of flying)	उड़ान (m)	urān
luggage	सामान (m)	sāmān

luggage cart	सामान के लिये गाड़ी (f)	sāmān ke liye gāṛī
ship	जहाज़ (m)	jahāz
cruise ship	लाइनर (m)	lainar
yacht	याख्ट (m)	yākht
boat (flat-bottomed ~)	नाव (m)	nāv
captain	कप्तान (m)	kaptān
cabin	कैबिन (m)	kaibin
port (harbor)	बंदरगाह (m)	bandaragāh
bicycle	साइकिल (f)	saikil
scooter	स्कूटर (m)	skūtar
motorcycle, bike	मोटरसाइकिल (f)	motarasaikil
pedal	पेडल (m)	pedal
pump	पंप (m)	pamp
wheel	पहिया (m)	pahiya
automobile, car	कार (f)	kār
ambulance	एम्बुलेंस (f)	embulens
truck	ट्रक (m)	trak
used (adj)	पुरानी	purānī
car crash	दुर्घटना (f)	durghatana
repair	मरम्मत (f)	marammat

11. Food. Part 1

meat	गोश्त (m)	gosht
chicken	चीकन (m)	chīkan
duck	बत्तख़ (f)	battakh
pork	सुअर का गोश्त (m)	suar ka gosht
veal	बछड़े का गोश्त (m)	bachhare ka gosht
lamb	भेड़ का गोश्त (m)	bher ka gosht
beef	गाय का गोश्त (m)	gāy ka gosht
sausage (bologna, pepperoni, etc.)	सॉसेज (f)	sosej
egg	अंडा (m)	anda
fish	मछली (f)	machhalī
cheese	पनीर (m)	panīr
sugar	चीनी (f)	chīnī
salt	नमक (m)	namak
rice	चावल (m)	chāval
pasta (macaroni)	पास्ता (m)	pāsta
butter	मक्खन (m)	makkhan
vegetable oil	तेल (m)	tel
bread	ब्रेड (f)	bred
chocolate (n)	चॉकलेट (m)	chokalet
wine	वाइन (f)	vain

coffee	कॉफ़ी (f)	kofī
milk	दूध (m)	dūdh
juice	रस (m)	ras
beer	बियर (m)	biyar
tea	चाय (f)	chāy

tomato	टमाटर (m)	tamātar
cucumber	खीरा (m)	khīra
carrot	गाजर (f)	gājar
potato	आलू (m)	ālū
onion	प्याज़ (m)	pyāz
garlic	लहसुन (m)	lahasun

cabbage	पत्ता गोभी (f)	patta gobhī
beetroot	चुकन्दर (m)	chukandar
eggplant	बैंगन (m)	baingan
dill	सोआ (m)	soa
lettuce	सलाद पत्ता (m)	salād patta
corn (maize)	मकई (f)	makī

fruit	फल (m)	fal
apple	सेब (m)	seb
pear	नाशपाती (f)	nāshapātī
lemon	नींबू (m)	nīmbū
orange	संतरा (m)	santara
strawberry (garden ~)	स्ट्रॉबेरी (f)	stroberī

plum	आलूबुखारा (m)	ālūbukhāra
raspberry	रसभरी (f)	rasabharī
pineapple	अनानास (m)	anānās
banana	केला (m)	kela
watermelon	तरबूज़ (m)	tarabūz
grape	अंगूर (m)	angūr
melon	खरबूज़ा (f)	kharabūza

12. Food. Part 2

cuisine	व्यंजन (m)	vyanjan
recipe	रैसीपी (f)	raisīpī
food	खाना (m)	khāna

to have breakfast	नाश्ता करना	nāshta karana
to have lunch	दोपहर का भोजन करना	dopahar ka bhojan karana
to have dinner	रात्रिभोज करना	rātribhoj karana

taste, flavor	स्वाद (m)	svād
tasty (adj)	स्वादिष्ट	svādisht
cold (adj)	ठंडा	thanda
hot (adj)	गरम	garam
sweet (sugary)	मीठा	mītha

salty (adj)	नमकीन	namakīn
sandwich (bread)	सैन्डविच (m)	saindavich
side dish	साइड डिश (f)	said dish
filling (for cake, pie)	फ़िलिंग (f)	filing
sauce	चटनी (f)	chatanī
piece (of cake, pie)	टुकड़ा (m)	tukara

diet	डाइट (m)	dait
vitamin	विटामिन (m)	vitāmin
calorie	कैलोरी (f)	kailorī
vegetarian (n)	शाकाहारी (m)	shākāhārī
restaurant	रेस्टराँ (m)	restarān
coffee house	कॉफ़ी हाउस (m)	kofī haus
appetite	भूख (f)	bhūkh
Enjoy your meal!	अपने भोजन का आनंद उठाए!	apane bhojan ka ānand uthaen!

waiter	बैरा (m)	baira
waitress	बैरी (f)	bairī
bartender	बारमैन (m)	bāramain
menu	मेनू (m)	menū

spoon	चम्मच (m)	chammach
knife	छुरी (f)	chhurī
fork	कांटा (m)	kānta
cup (e.g., coffee ~)	प्याला (m)	pyāla
plate (dinner ~)	तश्तरी (f)	tashtarī
saucer	सॉसर (m)	sosar
napkin (on table)	नैपकीन (m)	naipakīn
toothpick	टूथपिक (m)	tūthapik

to order (meal)	आर्डर देना	ārdar dena
course, dish	पकवान (m)	pakavān
portion	भाग (m)	bhāg
appetizer	एपेटाइज़र (m)	epetaizar
salad	सलाद (m)	salād
soup	सूप (m)	sūp

dessert	मीठा (m)	mītha
jam (whole fruit jam)	जैम (m)	jaim
ice-cream	आईस-क्रीम (f)	āīs-krīm

check	बिल (m)	bil
to pay the check	बील का भुगतान करना	bīl ka bhugatān karana
tip	टिप (f)	tip

13. House. Apartment. Part 1

| house | मकान (m) | makān |
| country house | गाँव का मकान (m) | gānv ka makān |

villa (seaside ~)	बंगला (m)	bangala
floor, story	मंज़िल (f)	manzil
entrance	प्रवेश-द्वार (m)	pravesh-dvār
wall	दीवार (f)	dīvār
roof	छत (f)	chhat
chimney	चिमनी (f)	chimanī
attic (storage place)	अटारी (f)	atārī
window	खिड़की (f)	khirakī
window ledge	विन्डो सिल (m)	vindo sil
balcony	बाल्कनी (f)	bālkanī
stairs (stairway)	सीढ़ी (f)	sīrhī
mailbox	लेटर बॉक्स (m)	letar boks
garbage can	कचरे का डब्बा (m)	kachare ka dabba
elevator	लिफ्ट (m)	lift
electricity	बिजली (f)	bijalī
light bulb	बल्ब (m)	balb
switch	स्विच (m)	svich
wall socket	सॉकेट (m)	soket
fuse	फ्यूज़ (m)	fyūz
door	दरवाज़ा (m)	daravāza
handle, doorknob	हत्था (m)	hattha
key	चाबी (f)	chābī
doormat	पायदान (m)	pāyadān
door lock	ताला (m)	tāla
doorbell	घंटी (f)	ghantī
knock (at the door)	खटखट (f)	khatakhat
to knock (vi)	खटखटाना	khatakhatāna
peephole	पीप होल (m)	pīp hol
yard	आंगन (m)	āngan
garden	बाग़ (m)	bāg
swimming pool	तरण-ताल (m)	taran-lāl
gym (home gym)	व्यायाम कक्ष (m)	vyāyām kaksh
tennis court	टेनिस-कोर्ट (m)	tenis-kort
garage	गराज (m)	garāj
private property	नीजी सम्पत्ति (f)	nījī sampatti
warning sign	चेतावनी संकेत (m)	chetāvanī sanket
security	सुरक्षा (f)	suraksha
security guard	पहरेदार (m)	paharedār
renovations	नवीकरण (m)	navīkaran
to renovate (vt)	नवीकरण करना	navīkaran karana
to put in order	ठीक करना	thīk karana
to paint (~ a wall)	रंगना	rangana
wallpaper	वॉल-पैपर (m pl)	vol-paipar
to varnish (vt)	पॉलिश करना	polish karana
pipe	पाइप (f)	paip

tools	औज़ार (m pl)	auzār
basement	तहख़ाना (m)	tahakhāna
sewerage (system)	मलप्रवाह-पद्धति (f)	malapravāh-paddhati

14. House. Apartment. Part 2

apartment	फ़्लैट (f)	flait
room	कमरा (m)	kamara
bedroom	सोने का कमरा (m)	sone ka kamara
dining room	खाने का कमरा (m)	khāne ka kamara

living room	बैठक (f)	baithak
study (home office)	घरेलू कार्यालय (m)	gharelū kāryālay
entry room	प्रवेश कक्ष (m)	pravesh kaksh
bathroom (room with a bath or shower)	स्नानघर (m)	snānaghar
half bath	शौचालय (m)	shauchālay

| floor | फ़र्श (m) | farsh |
| ceiling | छत (f) | chhat |

to dust (vt)	धूल पोंछना	dhūl ponchhana
vacuum cleaner	वैक्युम क्लीनर (m)	vaikyum klīnar
to vacuum (vt)	वैक्यूम करना	vaikyūm karana

mop	पोंछा (m)	ponchha
dust cloth	डस्टर (m)	dastar
short broom	झाड़ू (m)	jhārū
dustpan	कूड़ा उठाने का तसला (m)	kūra uthāne ka tasala

furniture	फ़र्निचर (m)	farnichar
table	मेज़ (f)	mez
chair	कुर्सी (f)	kursī
armchair	हत्थे वाली कुर्सी (f)	hatthe vālī kursī

bookcase	किताबों की अलमारी (f)	kitābon kī alamārī
shelf	शेल्फ़ (f)	shelf
wardrobe	कपड़ों की अलमारी (f)	kaparon kī alamārī

mirror	आईना (m)	āīna
carpet	कालीन (m)	kālīn
fireplace	चिमनी (f)	chimanī
drapes	परदे (m pl)	parade
table lamp	मेज़ का लैम्प (m)	mez ka laimp
chandelier	झूमर (m)	jhūmar

kitchen	रसोईघर (m)	rasoīghar
gas stove (range)	गैस का चूल्हा (m)	gais ka chūlha
electric stove	बिजली का चूल्हा (m)	bijalī ka chūlha
microwave oven	माइक्रोवेव ओवन (m)	maikrovev ovan

refrigerator	फ़ूज़ि (m)	frij
freezer	फ़्रीज़र (m)	frījar
dishwasher	डिशवॉशर (m)	dishavoshar
faucet	टोंटी (f)	tontī

meat grinder	कीमा बनाने की मशीन (f)	kīma banāne kī mashīn
juicer	जूसर (m)	jūsar
toaster	टोस्टर (m)	tostar
mixer	मिक्सर (m)	miksar

coffee machine	कॉफ़ी मशीन (f)	kofī mashīn
kettle	केतली (f)	ketalī
teapot	चायदानी (f)	chāyadānī

TV set	टीवी सेट (m)	tīvī set
VCR (video recorder)	वीडियो टेप रिकार्डर (m)	vīdiyo tep rikārdar
iron (e.g., steam ~)	इस्तरी (f)	istarī
telephone	टेलीफ़ोन (m)	telīfon

15. Professions. Social status

director	निदेशक (m)	nideshak
superior	वरिष्ठ अधिकारी (m)	varishth adhikārī
president	अध्यक्ष (m)	adhyaksh
assistant	सहायक (m)	sahāyak
secretary	सेक्रटरी (f)	sekratarī

owner, proprietor	मालिक (m)	mālik
partner	पार्टनर (m)	pārtanar
stockholder	शेयर होलडर (m)	sheyar holadar

businessman	व्यापारी (m)	vyāpārī
millionaire	लखपति (m)	lakhapati
billionaire	करोड़पति (m)	karorapati

actor	अभिनेता (m)	abhineta
architect	वास्तुकार (m)	vāstukār
banker	बैंकर (m)	bainkar
broker	ब्रोकर (m)	brokar

veterinarian	पशुचिकित्सक (m)	pashuchikitsak
doctor	चिकित्सक (m)	chikitsak
chambermaid	चैम्बरमेड (f)	chaimbaramed
designer	डिज़ाइनर (m)	dizainar
correspondent	पत्रकार (m)	patrakār
delivery man	कूरियर (m)	kūriyar

electrician	बिजलीवाला (m)	bijalīvāla
musician	साज़िन्दा (m)	sāzinda
babysitter	दाई (f)	daī

| hairdresser | नाई (m) | naī |
| herder, shepherd | चरवाहा (m) | charavāha |

singer (masc.)	गायक (m)	gāyak
translator	अनुवादक (m)	anuvādak
writer	लेखक (m)	lekhak
carpenter	बढ़ई (m)	barhī
cook	बावरची (m)	bāvarachī

fireman	दमकल कर्मचारी (m)	damakal karmachārī
police officer	पुलिसवाला (m)	pulisavāla
mailman	डाकिया (m)	dākiya
programmer	प्रोग्रामर (m)	progrāmar
salesman (store staff)	विक्रेता (m)	vikreta

worker	मज़दूर (m)	mazadūr
gardener	माली (m)	mālī
plumber	प्लम्बर (m)	plambar
dentist	दंतचिकित्सक (m)	dantachikitsak
flight attendant (fem.)	एयर होस्टेस (f)	eyar hostes

dancer (masc.)	नर्तक (m)	nartak
bodyguard	अंगरक्षक (m)	angarakshak
scientist	वैज्ञानिक (m)	vaigyānik
schoolteacher	शिक्षक (m)	shikshak

farmer	किसान (m)	kisān
surgeon	शल्य-चिकित्सक (m)	shaly-chikitsak
miner	खनिक (m)	khanik
chef (kitchen chef)	मुख्य बावरची (m)	mukhy bāvarachī
driver	ड्राइवर (m)	draivar

16. Sport

kind of sports	खेल (m)	khel
soccer	फुटबॉल (f)	futabol
hockey	हॉकी (f)	hokī
basketball	बास्केटबॉल (f)	bāsketabol
baseball	बेसबॉल (f)	besabol

volleyball	वॉलीबॉल (f)	volībol
boxing	मुक्केबाज़ी (f)	mukkebāzī
wrestling	कुश्ती (m)	kushtī
tennis	टेनिस (m)	tenis
swimming	तैराकी (m)	tairākī

chess	शतरंज (m)	shataranj
running	दौड़ (f)	daur
athletics	एथलेटिक्स (f)	ethaletiks
figure skating	फ़ीगर स्केटिन्ग (m)	fīgar sketing

cycling	साइकिलिंग (f)	saikiling
billiards	बिलियड्‍र्स (m)	biliyards
bodybuilding	बॉडीबिल्डिंग (m)	bodībilding
golf	गोल्फ़ (m)	golf
scuba diving	स्कूबा डाइविंग (f)	skūba daiving
sailing	पाल नौकायन (m)	pāl naukāyan
archery	तीरंदाज़ी (f)	tīrandāzī
period, half	हाफ़ (m)	hāf
half-time	हाफ़ टाइम (m)	hāf taim
tie	टाई (m)	taī
to tie (vi)	टाई करना	taī karana
treadmill	ट्रेडमिल (f)	tredamil
player	खिलाड़ी (m)	khilārī
substitute	रिज़र्व-खिलाड़ी (m)	rizarv-khilārī
substitutes bench	सब्सचिट्यूट बेंच (f)	sabsachityūt bench
match	मैच (m)	maich
goal	गोल (m)	gol
goalkeeper	गोलची (m)	golachī
goal (score)	गोल (m)	gol
Olympic Games	ओलिम्पिक खेल (m pl)	olimpik khel
to set a record	रिकॉर्ड बनाना	rikord banāna
final	फ़ाइनल (m)	fainal
champion	चेम्पियन (m)	chempiyan
championship	चैम्पियनशिप (f)	chaimpiyanaship
winner	विजेता (m)	vijeta
victory	विजय (m)	vijay
to win (vi)	जीतना	jītana
to lose (not win)	हारना	hārana
medal	मेडल (m)	medal
first place	पहला स्थान (m)	pahala sthān
second place	दूसरा स्थान (m)	dūsara sthān
third place	तीसरा स्थान (m)	tīsara sthān
stadium	स्टेडियम (m)	stediyam
fan, supporter	फ़ैन (m)	fain
trainer, coach	प्रशिक्षक (m)	prashikshak
training	प्रशिक्षण (f)	prashikshan

17. Foreign languages. Orthography

language	भाषा (f)	bhāsha
to study (vt)	पढ़ना	parhana
pronunciation	उच्चारण (m)	uchchāran
accent	लहज़ा (m)	lahaza

noun	संज्ञा (f)	sangya
adjective	विशेषण (m)	visheshan
verb	क्रिया (m)	kriya
adverb	क्रिया विशेषण (f)	kriya visheshan
pronoun	सर्वनाम (m)	sarvanām
interjection	विस्मयादिबोधक (m)	vismayādibodhak
preposition	पूर्वसर्ग (m)	pūrvasarg
root	मूल शब्द (m)	mūl shabd
ending	अन्त्याक्षर (m)	antyākshar
prefix	उपसर्ग (m)	upasarg
syllable	अक्षर (m)	akshar
suffix	प्रत्यय (m)	pratyay
stress mark	बल चिह्न (m)	bal chihn
period, dot	पूर्णविराम (m)	pūrnavirām
comma	उपविराम (m)	upavirām
colon	कोलन (m)	kolan
ellipsis	तीन बिन्दु (m)	tīn bindu
question	प्रश्न (m)	prashn
question mark	प्रश्न चिह्न (m)	prashn chihn
exclamation point	विस्मयादिबोधक चिह्न (m)	vismayādibodhak chihn
in quotation marks	उद्धरण चिह्न में	uddharan chihn men
in parenthesis	कोष्ठक में	koshthak men
letter	अक्षर (m)	akshar
capital letter	बड़ा अक्षर (m)	bara akshar
sentence	वाक्य (m)	vāky
group of words	शब्दों का समूह (m)	shabdon ka samūh
expression	अभिव्यक्ति (f)	abhivyakti
subject	कर्ता (m)	kartta
predicate	विधेय (m)	vidhey
line	पंक्ति (f)	pankti
paragraph	अनुच्छेद (m)	anuchchhed
synonym	समनार्थक शब्द (m)	samanārthak shabd
antonym	विपरीतार्थी शब्द (m)	viparītārthī shabd
exception	अपवाद (m)	apavād
to underline (vt)	रेखांकित करना	rekhānkit karana
rules	नियम (m pl)	niyam
grammar	व्याकरण (m)	vyākaran
vocabulary	शब्दावली (f)	shabdāvalī
phonetics	स्वरविज्ञान (m)	svaravigyān
alphabet	वर्णमाला (f)	varnamāla
textbook	पाठ्यपुस्तक (f)	pāthyapustak
dictionary	शब्दकोश (m)	shabdakosh

phrasebook	वार्त्तालाप-पुस्तिका (f)	vārttālāp-pustika
word	शब्द (m)	shabd
meaning	मतलब (m)	matalab
memory	स्मृति (f)	smrti

18. The Earth. Geography

the Earth	पृथ्वी (f)	prthvī
the globe (the Earth)	गोला (m)	gola
planet	ग्रह (m)	grah

geography	भूगोल (m)	bhūgol
nature	प्रकृति (f)	prakrti
map	नक्शा (m)	naksha
atlas	मानचित्रावली (f)	mānachitrāvalī

in the north	उत्तर में	uttar men
in the south	दक्षिण में	dakshin men
in the west	पश्चिम में	pashchim men
in the east	पूर्व में	pūrv men

sea	सागर (m)	sāgar
ocean	महासागर (m)	mahāsāgar
gulf (bay)	खाड़ी (f)	khārī
straits	जलग्रीवा (m)	jalagrīva

continent (mainland)	महाद्वीप (m)	mahādvīp
island	द्वीप (m)	dvīp
peninsula	प्रायद्वीप (m)	prāyadvīp
archipelago	द्वीप समूह (m)	dvīp samūh

harbor	बंदरगाह (m)	bandaragāh
coral reef	प्रवाल रीफ़ (m)	pravāl rīf
shore	किनारा (m)	kināra
coast	तटबंध (m)	tatabandh

| flow (flood tide) | ज्वार (m) | jvār |
| ebb (ebb tide) | भाटा (m) | bhāta |

latitude	अक्षांश (m)	akshānsh
longitude	देशान्तर (m)	deshāntar
parallel	समांतर-रेखा (f)	samāntar-rekha
equator	भूमध्य रेखा (f)	bhūmadhy rekha

sky	आकाश (f)	ākāsh
horizon	क्षितिज (m)	kshitij
atmosphere	वातावरण (m)	vātāvaran

| mountain | पहाड़ (m) | pahār |
| summit, top | चोटी (f) | chotī |

cliff	शिला (f)	shila
hill	टीला (m)	tīla
volcano	ज्वालामुखी (m)	jvālāmukhī
glacier	हिमनद (m)	himanad
waterfall	झरना (m)	jharana
plain	समतल प्रदेश (m)	samatal pradesh
river	नदी (f)	nadī
spring (natural source)	झरना (m)	jharana
bank (of river)	तट (m)	tat
downstream (adv)	बहाव के साथ	bahāv ke sāth
upstream (adv)	बहाव के विरुद्ध	bahāv ke virūddh
lake	तालाब (m)	tālāb
dam	बांध (m)	bāndh
canal	नहर (f)	nahar
swamp (marshland)	दलदल (f)	daladal
ice	बर्फ़ (m)	barf

19. Countries of the world. Part 1

Europe	यूरोप (m)	yūrop
European Union	यूरोपीय संघ (m)	yūropīy sangh
European (n)	यरोपीय (m)	yaropīy
European (adj)	यरोपीय	yaropīy
Austria	ऑस्ट्रिया (m)	ostriya
Great Britain	ग्रेट ब्रिटेन (m)	gret briten
England	इंग्लैंड (m)	inglaind
Belgium	बेल्जियम (m)	beljiyam
Germany	जर्मन (m)	jarman
Netherlands	नीदरलैंड्स (m)	nīdaralainds
Holland	हॉलैंड (m)	holaind
Greece	ग्रीस (m)	grīs
Denmark	डेन्मार्क (m)	denmārk
Ireland	आयरलैंड (m)	āyaralaind
Iceland	आयसलैंड (m)	āyasalaind
Spain	स्पेन (m)	spen
Italy	इटली (m)	italī
Cyprus	साइप्रस (m)	saipras
Malta	माल्टा (m)	mālta
Norway	नार्वे (m)	nārve
Portugal	पुर्तगाल (m)	purtagāl
Finland	फ़िनलैंड (m)	finalaind
France	फ़्रांस (m)	frāns
Sweden	स्वीडन (m)	svīdan

Switzerland	स्विट्ज़रलैंड (m)	svitzaralaind
Scotland	स्कॉटलैंड (m)	skotalaind
Vatican	वेटिकन (m)	vetikan
Liechtenstein	लिकटेंस्टीन (m)	likatenstīn
Luxembourg	लक्ज़मबर्ग (m)	lakzamabarg
Monaco	मोनाको (m)	monāko
Albania	अल्बानिया (m)	albāniya
Bulgaria	बुल्गारिया (m)	bulgāriya
Hungary	हंगरी (m)	hangarī
Latvia	लाटविया (m)	lātaviya
Lithuania	लिथुआनिया (m)	lithuāniya
Poland	पोलैंड (m)	polaind
Romania	रोमानिया (m)	romāniya
Serbia	सर्बिया (m)	sarbiya
Slovakia	स्लोवाकिया (m)	slovākiya
Croatia	क्रोएशिया (m)	kroeshiya
Czech Republic	चेक गणतंत्र (m)	chek ganatantr
Estonia	एस्तोनिया (m)	estoniya
Bosnia and Herzegovina	बोस्निया और हर्ज़ेगोविना	bosniya aur harzegovina
Macedonia (Republic of ~)	मेसेडोनिया (m)	mesedoniya
Slovenia	स्लोवेनिया (m)	sloveniya
Montenegro	मोंटेनेग्रो (m)	montenegro
Belarus	बेलारूस (m)	belārūs
Moldova, Moldavia	मोलदोवा (m)	moladova
Russia	रूस (m)	rūs
Ukraine	यूक्रेन (m)	yūkren

20. Countries of the world. Part 2

Asia	एशिया (f)	eshiya
Vietnam	वियतनाम (m)	viyatanām
India	भारत (m)	bhārat
Israel	इस्रायल (m)	isrāyal
China	चीन (m)	chīn
Lebanon	लेबनान (m)	lebanān
Mongolia	मंगोलिया (m)	mangoliya
Malaysia	मलेशिया (m)	maleshiya
Pakistan	पाकिस्तान (m)	pākistān
Saudi Arabia	सऊदी अरब (m)	saūdī arab
Thailand	थाईलैंड (m)	thaīlaind
Taiwan	ताइवान (m)	taivān
Turkey	तुर्की (m)	turkī
Japan	जापान (m)	jāpān
Afghanistan	अफ़ग़ानिस्तान (m)	afagānistān

Bangladesh	बांग्लादेश (m)	bānglādesh
Indonesia	इण्डोनेशिया (m)	indoneshiya
Jordan	जॉर्डन (m)	jordan
Iraq	इराक़ (m)	irāq
Iran	इरान (m)	irān

Cambodia	कम्बोडिया (m)	kambodiya
Kuwait	कुवैत (m)	kuvait
Laos	लाओस (m)	laos
Myanmar	म्यांमर (m)	myāmmar
Nepal	नेपाल (m)	nepāl

United Arab Emirates	संयुक्त अरब अमीरात (m)	sanyukt arab amīrāt
Syria	सीरिया (m)	sīriya
Palestine	फिलिस्तीन (m)	filistīn
South Korea	दक्षिण कोरिया (m)	dakshin koriya
North Korea	उत्तर कोरिया (m)	uttar koriya

United States of America	संयुक्त राज्य अमरीका (m)	sanyukt rājy amarīka
Canada	कनाडा (m)	kanāda
Mexico	मेक्सिको (m)	meksiko
Argentina	अर्जेंटीना (m)	arjentīna
Brazil	ब्राज़ील (m)	brāzīl

Colombia	कोलम्बिया (m)	kolambiya
Cuba	क्यूबा (m)	kyūba
Chile	चिली (m)	chilī
Venezuela	वेनेज़ुएला (m)	venezuela
Ecuador	इक्वेडोर (m)	ikvedor

The Bahamas	बहामा (m)	bahāma
Panama	पनामा (m)	panāma
Egypt	मिस्र (m)	misr
Morocco	मोरक्को (m)	morakko
Tunisia	ट्युनीसिया (m)	tyunīsiya

Kenya	केन्या (m)	kenya
Libya	लीबिया (m)	lībiya
South Africa	दक्षिण अफ्रीका (m)	dakshin afrīka
Australia	आस्ट्रेलिया (m)	āstreliya
New Zealand	न्यू ज़ीलैंड (m)	nyū zīlaind

21. Weather. Natural disasters

weather	मौसम (m)	mausam
weather forecast	मौसम का पूर्वानुमान (m)	mausam ka pūrvānumān
temperature	तापमान (m)	tāpamān
thermometer	थर्मामीटर (m)	tharmāmītar
barometer	बैरोमीटर (m)	bairomītar
sun	सूरज (m)	sūraj

to shine (vi)	चमकना	chamakana
sunny (day)	धूपदार	dhūpadār
to come up (vi)	उगना	ugana
to set (vi)	डूबना	dūbana

rain	बारिश (f)	bārish
it's raining	बारिश हो रही है	bārish ho rahī hai
pouring rain	मूसलधार बारिश (f)	mūsaladhār bārish
rain cloud	घना बादल (m)	ghana bādal
puddle	पोखर (m)	pokhar
to get wet (in rain)	भीगना	bhīgana

thunderstorm	गरजवाला तुफान (m)	garajavāla tufān
lightning (~ strike)	बिजली (m)	bijalī
to flash (vi)	चमकना	chamakana
thunder	गरज (m)	garaj
it's thundering	बादल गरज रहा है	bādal garaj raha hai
hail	ओला (m)	ola
it's hailing	ओले पड़ रहे हैं	ole par rahe hain

heat (extreme ~)	गरमी (f)	garamī
it's hot	गरमी है	garamī hai
it's warm	गरम है	garam hai
it's cold	ठंडक है	thandak hai

fog (mist)	कुहरा (m)	kuhara
foggy	कुहरेदार	kuharedār
cloud	बादल (m)	bādal
cloudy (adj)	मेघाच्छादित	meghāchchhādit
humidity	नमी (f)	namī

snow	बर्फ़ (f)	barf
it's snowing	बर्फ़ पड़ रही है	barf par rahī hai
frost (severe ~, freezing cold)	पाला (m)	pāla
below zero (adv)	शून्य से नीचे	shūny se nīche
hoarfrost	पाला (m)	pāla

bad weather	ख़राब मौसम (m)	kharāb mausam
disaster	प्रलय (m)	pralay
flood, inundation	बाढ़ (f)	bārh
avalanche	हिमस्खलन (m)	himaskhalan
earthquake	भूकंप (m)	bhūkamp

tremor, quake	झटका (m)	jhataka
epicenter	अधिकेंद्र (m)	adhikendr
eruption	उद्गार (m)	udgār
lava	लावा (m)	lāva

tornado	टोर्नेडो (m)	tornedo
twister	बवंडर (m)	bavandar
hurricane	समुद्री तूफ़ान (m)	samudrī tūfān

| tsunami | सुनामी (f) | sunāmī |
| cyclone | चक्रवात (m) | chakravāt |

22. Animals. Part 1

| animal | जानवर (m) | jānavar |
| predator | परभक्षी (m) | parabhakshī |

tiger	बाघ (m)	bāgh
lion	शेर (m)	sher
wolf	भेड़िया (m)	bheriya
fox	लोमड़ी (f)	lomri
jaguar	जागुआर (m)	jāguār

lynx	वन बिलाव (m)	van bilāv
coyote	कोयोट (m)	koyot
jackal	गीदड़ (m)	gīdar
hyena	लकड़बग्घा (m)	lakarabaggha

squirrel	गिलहरी (f)	gilaharī
hedgehog	कांटा-चूहा (m)	kānta-chūha
rabbit	खरगोश (m)	kharagosh
raccoon	रैकून (m)	raikūn

hamster	हैम्स्टर (m)	haimstar
mole	छछूंदर (m)	chhachhūndar
mouse	चूहा (m)	chūha
rat	घूस (m)	ghūs
bat	चमगादड़ (m)	chamagādar

beaver	ऊदबिलाव (m)	ūdabilāv
horse	घोड़ा (m)	ghora
deer	हिरण (m)	hiran
camel	ऊंट (m)	ūnt
zebra	ज़ेबरा (m)	zebara

whale	ह्वेल (f)	hvel
seal	सील (m)	sīl
walrus	वॉलरस (m)	volaras
dolphin	डॉलफ़िन (f)	dolafin

bear	रीछ (m)	rīchh
monkey	बंदर (m)	bandar
elephant	हाथी (m)	hāthī
rhinoceros	गैंडा (m)	gainda
giraffe	जिराफ़ (m)	jirāf

hippopotamus	दरियाई घोड़ा (m)	dariyaī ghora
kangaroo	कंगारू (m)	kangārū
cat	बिल्ली (f)	billī

dog	कुत्ता (m)	kutta
cow	गाय (f)	gāy
bull	बैल (m)	bail
sheep (ewe)	भेड़ (f)	bher
goat	बकरी (f)	bakarī
donkey	गधा (m)	gadha
pig, hog	सुअर (m)	suar
hen (chicken)	मुर्गी (f)	murgī
rooster	मुर्गा (m)	murga
duck	बतख़ (f)	battakh
goose	हंस (m)	hans
turkey (hen)	टर्की (f)	tarkī
sheepdog	गड़रिये का कुत्ता (m)	garariye ka kutta

23. Animals. Part 2

bird	चिड़िया (f)	chiriya
pigeon	कबूतर (m)	kabūtar
sparrow	गौरैया (f)	gauraiya
tit (great tit)	टिटरी (f)	titarī
magpie	नीलकण्ठ पक्षी (f)	nīlakanth pakshī
eagle	चील (f)	chīl
hawk	बाज़ (m)	bāz
falcon	बाज़ (m)	bāz
swan	राजहंस (m)	rājahans
crane	सारस (m)	sāras
stork	लकलक (m)	lakalak
parrot	तोता (m)	tota
peacock	मोर (m)	mor
ostrich	शुतुरमुर्ग (m)	shuturamurg
heron	बगुला (m)	bagula
nightingale	बुलबुल (m)	bulabul
swallow	अबाबील (f)	abābīl
woodpecker	कठफोड़ा (m)	kathafora
cuckoo	कोयल (f)	koyal
owl	उल्लू (m)	ullū
penguin	पेंगुइन (m)	penguin
tuna	टूना (f)	tūna
trout	ट्रॉउट (f)	traut
eel	सर्पमीन (f)	sarpamīn
shark	शार्क (f)	shārk
crab	केकड़ा (m)	kekara
jellyfish	जेली फ़िश (f)	jelī fish

octopus	आक्टोपस (m)	āktopas
starfish	स्टार फ़िश (f)	stār fish
sea urchin	जलसाही (f)	jalasāhī
seahorse	समुद्री घोड़ा (m)	samudrī ghora
shrimp	झींगा (f)	jhīnga
snake	सर्प (m)	sarp
viper	वाइपर (m)	vaipar
lizard	छिपकली (f)	chhipakalī
iguana	इग्यूएना (m)	igyūena
chameleon	गिरगिट (m)	giragit
scorpion	वृश्चिक (m)	vrshchik
turtle	कछुआ (m)	kachhua
frog	मेंढक (m)	mendhak
crocodile	मगर (m)	magar
insect, bug	कीट (m)	kīt
butterfly	तितली (f)	titalī
ant	चींटी (f)	chīntī
fly	मक्खी (f)	makkhī
mosquito	मच्छर (m)	machchhar
beetle	भृंग (m)	bhrng
bee	मधुमक्खी (f)	madhumakkhī
spider	मकड़ी (f)	makarī

24. Trees. Plants

tree	पेड़ (m)	per
birch	सनोबर का पेड़ (m)	sanobar ka per
oak	बलूत (m)	balūt
linden tree	लिनडेन वृक्ष (m)	linaden vrksh
aspen	आस्पेन वृक्ष (m)	āspen vrksh
maple	मेपल (m)	mepal
spruce	फर का पेड़ (m)	far ka per
pine	देवदार (m)	devadār
cedar	देवदर (m)	devadar
poplar	पोप्लर वृक्ष (m)	poplar vrksh
rowan	रोवाण (m)	rovān
beech	बीच (m)	bīch
elm	एल्म वृक्ष (m)	elm vrksh
ash (tree)	एश-वृक्ष (m)	esh-vrksh
chestnut	चेस्टनट (m)	chestanat
palm tree	ताड़ का पेड़ (m)	tār ka per
bush	झाड़ी (f)	jhārī
mushroom	गगन-धूलि (f)	gagan-dhūli

poisonous mushroom	ज़हरीली गगन-धूलि (f)	zaharīlī gagan-dhūli
cep (Boletus edulis)	सफ़ेद गगन-धूलि (f)	safed gagan-dhūli
russula	रसुला (f)	rasula
fly agaric	फ्लाई ऐगेरिक (f)	flaī aigerik
death cap	डेथ कैप (f)	deth kaip

flower	फूल (m)	fūl
bouquet (of flowers)	गुलदस्ता (m)	guladasta
rose (flower)	गुलाब (f)	gulāb
tulip	ट्यूलिप (m)	tyūlip
carnation	गुलनार (m)	gulanār

camomile	कैमोमाइल (m)	kaimomail
cactus	कैक्टस (m)	kaiktas
lily of the valley	कामुदिनी (f)	kāmudinī
snowdrop	सफ़ेद फूल (m)	safed fūl
water lily	कुमुदिनी (f)	kumudinī

greenhouse (tropical ~)	शीशाघर (m)	shīshāghar
lawn	घास का मैदान (m)	ghās ka maidān
flowerbed	फुलवारी (f)	fulavārī

plant	पौधा (m)	paudha
grass	घास (f)	ghās
leaf	पत्ती (f)	pattī
petal	पंखड़ी (f)	pankharī
stem	डंडी (f)	dandī
young plant (shoot)	अंकुर (m)	ankur

cereal crops	अनाज की फ़सलें (m pl)	anāj kī fasalen
wheat	गेहूं (m)	gehūn
rye	रई (f)	raī
oats	जई (f)	jaī

millet	बाजरा (m)	bājara
barley	जौ (m)	jau
corn	मक्का (m)	makka
rice	चावल (m)	chāval

25. Various useful words

balance (of situation)	संतुलन (m)	santulan
base (basis)	आधार (m)	ādhār
beginning	शुरू (m)	shurū
category	श्रेणी (f)	shrenī

choice	चुनाव (m)	chunāv
coincidence	समकालीनता (f)	samakālīnata
comparison	तुलना (f)	tulana
degree (extent, amount)	मात्रा (f)	mātra

development	विकास (m)	vikās
difference	फ़र्क़ (m)	fark
effect (e.g., of drugs)	प्रभाव (m)	prabhāv
effort (exertion)	प्रयत्न (m)	prayatn
element	तत्व (m)	tatv
example (illustration)	उदाहरण (m)	udāharan
fact	तथ्य (m)	tathy
help	सहायता (f)	sahāyata
ideal	आदर्श (m)	ādarsh
kind (sort, type)	प्रकार (m)	prakār
mistake, error	ग़लती (f)	galatī
moment	पल (m)	pal
obstacle	अवरोध (m)	avarodh
part (~ of sth)	भाग (m)	bhāg
pause (break)	विराम (m)	virām
position	स्थिति (f)	sthiti
problem	समस्या (f)	samasya
process	प्रक्रिया (f)	prakriya
progress	उन्नति (f)	unnati
property (quality)	गुण (m)	gun
reaction	प्रतिक्रिया (f)	pratikriya
risk	जोखिम (m)	jokhim
secret	रहस्य (m)	rahasy
series	श्रृंखला (f)	shrrnkhala
shape (outer form)	रूप (m)	rūp
situation	स्थिति (f)	sthiti
solution	हल (m)	hal
standard (adj)	मानक	mānak
stop (pause)	विराम (m)	virām
style	शैली (f)	shailī
system	प्रणाली (f)	pranālī
table (chart)	सारणी (f)	sāranī
tempo, rate	गति (f)	gati
term (word, expression)	पारिभाषिक शब्द (m)	pāribhāshik shabd
truth (e.g., moment of ~)	सच (m)	sach
turn (please wait your ~)	बारी (f)	bārī
urgent (adj)	अत्यावश्यक	atyāvashyak
utility (usefulness)	उपयोग (m)	upayog
variant (alternative)	विकल्प (m)	vikalp
way (means, method)	तरीका (m)	tarīka
zone	क्षेत्र (m)	kshetr

26. Modifiers. Adjectives. Part 1

additional (adj)	अतिरिक्त	atirikt
ancient (~ civilization)	प्राचीन	prāchīn
artificial (adj)	कृत्रिम	krtrim
bad (adj)	बुरा	bura
beautiful (person)	सुंदर	sundar
big (in size)	बड़ा	bara
bitter (taste)	कड़वा	karava
blind (sightless)	अंधा	andha
central (adj)	केंद्रीय	kendrīy
children's (adj)	बच्चों का	bachchon ka
clandestine (secret)	गुप्त	gupt
clean (free from dirt)	साफ़	sāf
clever (smart)	बुद्धिमान	buddhimān
compatible (adj)	अनुकूल	anukūl
contented (satisfied)	संतुष्ट	santusht
dangerous (adj)	खतरनाक	khataranāk
dead (not alive)	मृत	mrt
dense (fog, smoke)	घना	ghana
difficult (decision)	मुश्किल	mushkil
dirty (not clean)	मैला	maila
easy (not difficult)	आसान	āsān
empty (glass, room)	खाली	khālī
exact (amount)	ठीक	thīk
excellent (adj)	उत्कृष्ट	utkrsht
excessive (adj)	अत्यधिक	atyadhik
exterior (adj)	बाहरी	bāharī
fast (quick)	तेज़	tez
fertile (land, soil)	उपजाऊ	upajaū
fragile (china, glass)	नाज़ुक	nāzuk
free (at no cost)	मुफ़्त	muft
fresh (~ water)	ताज़ा	tāza
frozen (food)	जमा	jama
full (completely filled)	भरा	bhara
happy (adj)	प्रसन्न	prasann
hard (not soft)	कड़ा	kara
huge (adj)	विशाल	vishāl
ill (sick, unwell)	बीमार	bīmār
immobile (adj)	अचल	achal
important (adj)	महत्वपूर्ण	mahatvapūrn
interior (adj)	आंतरिक	āntarik
last (e.g., ~ week)	पिछला	pichhala

last (final)	आखिरी	ākhirī
left (e.g., ~ side)	बायाँ	bāyān
legal (legitimate)	कानूनी	kānūnī

light (in weight)	हल्का	halka
liquid (fluid)	तरल	taral
long (e.g., ~ hair)	लंबा	lamba
loud (voice, etc.)	ऊंचा	ūncha
low (voice)	धीमा	dhīma

27. Modifiers. Adjectives. Part 2

main (principal)	मुख्य	mukhy
matt, matte	मैट	mait
mysterious (adj)	रहस्यपूर्ण	rahasyapūrn
narrow (street, etc.)	तंग	tang
native (~ country)	देसी	desī

negative (~ response)	नकारात्मक	nakārātmak
new (adj)	नया	naya
next (e.g., ~ week)	अगला	agala
normal (adj)	साधारण	sādhāran
not difficult (adj)	आसान	āsān

obligatory (adj)	अनिवार्य	anivāry
old (house)	पुराना	purāna
open (adj)	खुला	khula
opposite (adj)	उल्टा	ulta
ordinary (usual)	आम	ām

original (unusual)	मूल	mūl
personal (adj)	व्यक्तिगत	vyaktigat
polite (adj)	विनम्र	vinamr
poor (not rich)	गरीब	garīb

possible (adj)	संभव	sambhav
principal (main)	मूल	mūl
probable (adj)	मुमकिन	mumakin
prolonged (e.g., ~ applause)	दीर्घकालिक	dīrghakālik
public (open to all)	सार्वजनिक	sārvajanik

rare (adj)	असाधारण	asādhāran
raw (uncooked)	कच्चा	kachcha
right (not left)	दायां	dāyān
ripe (fruit)	पक्का	pakka

risky (adj)	खतरनाक	khataranāk
sad (~ look)	उदास	udās
second hand (adj)	इस्तेमाल किया हुआ	istemāl kiya hua

shallow (water)	उथला	uthala
sharp (blade, etc.)	तेज़	tez
short (in length)	छोटा	chhota
similar (adj)	मिलता-जुलता	milata-julata
small (in size)	छोटा	chhota
smooth (surface)	समतल	samatal
soft (~ toys)	नरम	naram
solid (~ wall)	मज़बूत	mazabūt
sour (flavor, taste)	खट्टा	khatta
spacious (house, etc.)	विस्तृत	vistrt
special (adj)	ख़ास	khās
straight (line, road)	सीधा	sīdha
strong (person)	शक्तिशाली	shaktishālī
stupid (foolish)	बेवकूफ़	bevakūf
superb, perfect (adj)	उत्तम	uttam
sweet (sugary)	मीठा	mītha
tan (adj)	सांवला	sānvala
tasty (delicious)	मज़ेदार	mazedār
unclear (adj)	धुंधला	dhundhala

28. Verbs. Part 1

to accuse (vt)	आरोप लगाना	ārop lagāna
to agree (say yes)	राज़ी होना	rāzī hona
to announce (vt)	घोषणा करना	ghoshana karana
to answer (vi, vt)	जवाब देना	javāb dena
to apologize (vi)	माफ़ी मांगना	māfī māngana
to arrive (vi)	पहुँचना	pahunchana
to ask (~ oneself)	पूछना	pūchhana
to be absent	अनुपस्थित होना	anupasthit hona
to be afraid	डरना	darana
to be born	जन्म होना	janm hona
to be in a hurry	जल्दी में रहना	jaldī men rahana
to beat (to hit)	पीटना	pītana
to begin (vt)	शुरू करना	shurū karana
to believe (in God)	आस्था रखना	āstha rakhana
to belong to ...	स्वामी होना	svāmī hona
to break (split into pieces)	तोड़ना	torana
to build (vt)	निर्माण करना	nirmān karana
to buy (purchase)	खरीदना	kharīdana
can (v aux)	सकना	sakana
can (v aux)	सकना	sakana
to cancel (call off)	रद्द करना	radd karana

to catch (vt)	पकड़ना	pakarana
to change (vt)	बदलना	badalana
to check (to examine)	जांचना	jānchana
to choose (select)	चुनना	chunana
to clean up (tidy)	साफ़ करना	sāf karana
to close (vt)	बंद करना	band karana
to compare (vt)	तुलना करना	tulana karana
to complain (vi, vt)	शिकायत करना	shikāyat karana
to confirm (vt)	पुष्टि करना	pushti karana
to congratulate (vt)	बधाई देना	badhaī dena
to cook (dinner)	खाना बनाना	khāna banāna
to copy (vt)	कॉपी करना	kopī karana
to cost (vt)	दाम होना	dām hona
to count (add up)	गिनना	ginana
to count on ...	भरोसा रखना	bharosa rakhana
to create (vt)	बनाना	banāna
to cry (weep)	रोना	rona
to dance (vi, vt)	नाचना	nāchana
to deceive (vi, vt)	धोखा देना	dhokha dena
to decide (~ to do sth)	फ़ैसला करना	faisala karana
to delete (vt)	हटाना	hatāna
to demand (request firmly)	माँगना	māngana
to deny (vt)	नकारना	nakārana
to depend on ...	निर्भर होना	nirbhar hona
to despise (vt)	नफ़रत करना	nafarat karana
to die (vi)	मरना	marana
to dig (vt)	खोदना	khodana
to disappear (vi)	ग़ायब हो जाना	gāyab ho jāna
to discuss (vt)	चर्चा करना	charcha karana
to disturb (vt)	परेशान करना	pareshān karana

29. Verbs. Part 2

to dive (vi)	डुबकी मारना	dubakī mārana
to divorce (vi)	तलाक़ देना	talāq dena
to do (vt)	करना	karana
to doubt (have doubts)	शक करना	shak karana
to drink (vi, vt)	पीना	pīna
to drop (let fall)	गिराना	girāna
to dry (clothes, hair)	सुखाना	sukhāna
to eat (vi, vt)	खाना खाना	khāna khāna
to end (~ a relationship)	ख़त्म करना	khatm karana
to excuse (forgive)	माफ़ करना	māf karana
to exist (vi)	होना	hona

to expect (foresee)	उम्मीद करना	ummīd karana
to explain (vt)	समझाना	samajhāna
to fall (vi)	गिरना	girana
to fight (street fight, etc.)	झगड़ना	jhagarana
to find (vt)	ढूढना	dhūṛhana
to finish (vt)	ख़त्म करना	khatm karana
to fly (vi)	उड़ना	urana
to forbid (vt)	प्रतिबंधित करना	pratibandhit karana
to forget (vi, vt)	भूलना	bhūlana
to forgive (vt)	क्षमा करना	kshama karana
to get tired	थकना	thakana
to give (vt)	देना	dena
to go (on foot)	जाना	jāna
to hate (vt)	नफ़रत करना	nafarat karana
to have (vt)	होना	hona
to have breakfast	नाश्ता करना	nāshta karana
to have dinner	रात्रिभोज करना	rātribhoj karana
to have lunch	दोपहर का भोजन करना	dopahar ka bhojan karana
to hear (vt)	सुनना	sunana
to help (vt)	मदद करना	madad karana
to hide (vt)	छिपाना	chhipāna
to hope (vi, vt)	आशा करना	āsha karana
to hunt (vi, vt)	शिकार करना	shikār karana
to hurry (vi)	जल्दी करना	jaldī karana
to insist (vi, vt)	आग्रह करना	āgrah karana
to insult (vt)	अपमान करना	apamān karana
to invite (vt)	आमंत्रित करना	āmantrit karana
to joke (vi)	मज़ाक करना	mazāk karana
to keep (vt)	रखना	rakhana
to kill (vt)	मार डालना	mār ḍālana
to know (sb)	जानना	jānana
to know (sth)	मालूम होना	mālūm hona
to like (I like …)	पसंद करना	pasand karana
to look at …	देखना	dekhana
to lose (umbrella, etc.)	खोना	khona
to love (sb)	प्यार करना	pyār karana
to make a mistake	गलती करना	galatī karana
to meet (vi, vt)	मिलना	milana
to miss (school, etc.)	ग़ैर-हाज़िर होना	gair-hāzir hona

30. Verbs. Part 3

to obey (vi, vt)	मानना	mānana
to open (vt)	खोलना	kholana

to participate (vi)	भाग लेना	bhāg lena
to pay (vi, vt)	दाम चुकाना	dām chukāna
to permit (vt)	अनुमति देना	anumati dena
to play (children)	खेलना	khelana
to pray (vi, vt)	दुआ देना	dua dena
to promise (vt)	वचन देना	vachan dena
to propose (vt)	प्रस्ताव रखना	prastāv rakhana
to prove (vt)	साबित करना	sābit karana
to read (vi, vt)	पढ़ना	parhana
to receive (vt)	पाना	pāna
to rent (sth from sb)	किराए पर लेना	kirae par lena
to repeat (say again)	दोहराना	doharāna
to reserve, to book	बुक करना	buk karana
to run (vi)	दौड़ना	daurana
to save (rescue)	बचाना	bachāna
to say (~ thank you)	कहना	kahana
to see (vt)	देखना	dekhana
to sell (vt)	बेचना	bechana
to send (vt)	भेजना	bhejana
to shoot (vi)	गोली चलाना	golī chalāna
to shout (vi)	चिल्लाना	chillāna
to show (vt)	दिखाना	dikhāna
to sign (document)	हस्ताक्षर करना	hastākshar karana
to sing (vi)	गाना	gāna
to sit down (vi)	बैठना	baithana
to smile (vi)	मुस्कुराना	muskurāna
to speak (vi, vt)	बोलना	bolana
to steal (money, etc.)	चुराना	churāna
to stop (please ~ calling me)	बंद करना	band karana
to study (vt)	पढ़ाई करना	parhaī karana
to swim (vi)	तैरना	tairana
to take (vt)	लेना	lena
to talk to …	से कहना	se kahana
to tell (story, joke)	बताना	batāna
to thank (vt)	धन्यवाद देना	dhanyavād dena
to think (vi, vt)	सोचना	sochana
to translate (vt)	अनुवाद करना	anuvād karana
to trust (vt)	यकीन करना	yakīn karana
to try (attempt)	कोशिश करना	koshish karana
to turn (e.g., ~ left)	मुड़ जाना	mur jāna
to turn off	बंद करना	band karana
to turn on	चलाना	chalāna
to understand (vt)	समझना	samajhana

to wait (vt)	इंतज़ार करना	intazār karana
to want (wish, desire)	चाहना	chāhana
to work (vi)	काम करना	kām karana
to write (vt)	लिखना	likhana

www.ingramcontent.com/pod-product-compliance
Lightning Source LLC
Chambersburg PA
CBHW060023050426
42448CB00012B/2856